The Medieval Inquisition

Albert C. Shannon, O.S.A.

Second Edition

A Michael Glazier Book
THE LITURGICAL PRESS
Collegeville, Minnesota

A Michael Glazier Book published by The Liturgical Press.

Cover design by David Manahan, O.S.B.

1 2 3 4 5 6 7 8 9

Library of Congress Cataloging-in-Publication Data

Shannon, Albert Clement, 1918–
The medieval Inquisition / Albert C. Shannon. — 2nd ed.
p. cm.
"A Michael Glazier book."
Includes bibliographical references.
ISBN 0-8146-5779-6
1. Inquisition. 2. Church history—Middle Ages, 600–1500.
I. Title.
BX1712.S53 1991
272'.2—dc20 91-22659
CIP

For

Austin Patterson Evans

and

Lynn Thorndike

CONTENTS

FOREWORD

The mere mention of the words 'heresy' and 'inquisition' in this day and age is sufficient to raise the hackles of a great many people. And if 'medieval' and 'papal' are added, the displeasure is almost palpable. Why this should be is not difficult to discover. Textbooks through the years have painted a rather dismal picture of these events, and, despite the ecumenical spirit of the times, most people have been taught something of the origins of their religions and the differences and conflicts that have been associated with their history. Strange as it may seem, this burgeoning interest shows itself most dramatically in the scholarly world itself, for, as one authority has noted, more than 2,000 books, monographs, and articles have appeared on this subject since 1960.

The literature on the Inquisition is, then, extensive and expanding. What is even more astounding is that with all this research, scholarly agreement has not significantly increased. On the contrary, sharp differences mark the discussion of practically every point. This is not so much because of religious passions as in the olden times, for the academic community is anything but religious; in fact this is a major stumbling block. But rather it would seem to be caused by the diverse explanations of the historical events themselves: not so much what happened, although there is no lack of problems here, but rather how and why these occurrences developed. The contemporary chroniclers, William of Puylaurens, William Pelhisson, Peter of Les Vaux de Cernay, William of Tudela, Walter Map are helpful but often lack objectivity and accuracy. Events are colored by the current state of the relations between the Papacy and the Empire; the struggles of the Guelphs (cities in Italy that supported the Papacy) and the Ghibellines (allies of the Emperor); the rivalries among the cities themselves and of parties within the cities; in France, the overlapping allegiances of the higher nobility to the King of France, the King of Aragon, and the Emperor, compounded by the struggles both of the lesser nobility and of the towns with the Counts, and the general unstable and evolving political situation in Languedoc. Further, the medieval cavalier attitude toward numbers (soldiers, heretics, killed, confiscations, etc.) must be reckoned with, though they have no monopoly on that abberration: witness the statement of a modern authority that "7,000 women, children and old people were massacred in the church of La Madeleine"[1] at Béziers - some church!

So extensive is the continuing flood of works on various phases of the Inquisition that individual compilations have been published just to keep up with the bibliography, e.g., *Bibliographie zur Ketzergeschichte des Mittelalters (1900-1966)* by Herbert Grundmann; *Bibliographie der Inquisition* by Emil van der Vekené (1963); "A Survey of Recent Research on the Albigensian Cathari," in *Church History* by Daniel Walther (1965); "Interpretations of the Origins of Medieval Heresy," in *Medieval Studies* by Jeffrey Russell (1963); *Medieval Heresy, Popular Movements from Bogomil to Hus,* by Malcolm Lambert (1976); *Bibliographie du catharisme languedocien* by Pierre de Berne-Lagarde (1957); "La Contribution des ouvrages critiques récents à l'histoire de l'hérésie méridionale," in the *Bulletin de la Société ariégeoise des sciences, lettres et artes* by Jean Duvernoy (1968); *Bibliografia valdese* by Augusto Armand-Hugon and Giovanni Gonnet (1953); *Historiographie du catharisme,* no. 14 of *Cahiers de Fanjeaux* (1979); *Medieval Heresies, a Bibliography 1960-1979,* by Carl T. Berkhout and Jeffrey B. Russell (1981). A regular series is published of current discussions on thirteenth century religious history of Languedoc, the *Cahiers de Fanjeaux;* another continuing publication deals with the Cathars, the *Cahiers d'études cathares;* still others with the Waldensians, *Bulletin de la Société d'histoire vaudoise; Bolletino della Società de studi valdesi.* And the list could go on almost endlessly.

An overview of heresy and the Inquisition in thirteenth

century France, then, would seem to be of special interest to the general public. For the academic community the problem is considerably more complex as indicated by Professor C.N.L. Brooke:

> The new situation [freedom of belief] is the product (so far as one can understand a very complex and obscure process of causation) of the spread of tolerance, of humane and liberal sentiment, in recent centuries; and also of the revolution in intellectual climate which means that countless men and women today think there is nothing ultimately obscure about the world, or (which can be a very different thing) nothing makes the notion of a divine creator or saviour either necessary or plausible. This last situation, the confident rationalism or the scientifically based agnosticism which have come to be the dominant faiths among the twentieth century intellectuals, were indeed unthinkable in the twelfth century at least in any recognisable form.[2]

A similar point of view is expressed by Professor John Mundy:

> It is obvious that doubt and scepticism were significant parts of the Latin view of the world. What held them in check, one feels, was not the capacity of churchmen to prove personal resurrection, free will, man's freedom to make moral choices, and other like propositions. These things can be hoped for or believed in, but, as not a few of the theologians and philosophers of the time stated [sic] they cannot be proved.[3]

Taken at face value this dictum can only mean that no one then, or now, could be required to obey the law, much less would it be just to punish him for breaking the law, since freedom of the human will, personal responsibility, is the irreducible condition for all law. If, then, this is the attitude of academicians, one can fathom their disdain in trying to appreciate a medieval civilization that did believe in a personal God and a people to whom God was a very real part of their lives, Who in the Person of Christ had established a church to teach them His way of life leading to eternal salvation, a people who did hold each other morally responsible for one's own acts.

Our discussion of heresy and the Inquisition will be circumscribed in time by the thirteenth century, and by place to southern France, Languedoc. The Inquisition was formally established by Pope Gregory IX in 1231/33, and the main heresy, Albigensianism, had to all intents and purposes run its course by the end of the century. There were, it is true, individual Inquisitors in Germany and in northern Italy, but not in an organized, centralized basis as in the Midi. While the Inquisition did linger into the fourteenth century, heresy, as exemplified by the Waldensians, generally retreated to isolated places. It was felt that the present and urgent danger had passed.

In the flowering of Christendom at this period the common heritage of all social ranks in western Europe was Roman Catholicism. When one spoke of the Faith, Christianity, the Church, all understood that these terms applied solely to the teachings of the Catholic Church. Although there were individual heresiarchs, leaders of particular groups, the only two organized sects with a large continuing following were the Albigensians and the Waldensians. Since they both claimed to be Christian, to the extent that their teachings differed from the Roman Church they were considered to be heretics in the popular mind. On the other hand since neither the Jews nor the pagans purported to be Christian, they were not accounted heretics. Further, we are not here concerned with the so-called Spanish Inquisition which originated some two centuries later and was dominated by the Spanish crown for quite different purposes.[4] Since the Albigensians and the Waldensians directly challenged the unity of faith of Roman Catholicism our task in the First Chapter of this study will be to outline their beliefs and practices in contrast to the traditional teachings of the Roman Church. It seemed to me that the fairest and most objective way to present the teachings of each of the three religions was to permit each party to state its own case in so far as historically possible from contemporary documents, and not in a polemical or adversary way. Thus, the Albigensian and Waldensian doctrines are taken from a late twelfth or early thirteenth century treatise, *The Summa Contra Haereticos Ascribed to Praepositinus of Cremona,* while the Roman Catholic position is quoted from the first and third canons of the Fourth Lateran Council of 1215. In order that the differences in doctrine may be more easily compared, a tabular chart of the principal teachings of the three religious bodies concludes the Chapter.

Chapter Two recreates the Medieval World of Christendom which was sustained by the close interdependence of Church and State, in which the anti-ecclesiastical and anti-social nature of the two heresies was regarded by all as a pressing and urgent danger. The attempts of the Church to deal with the dissident sects by persuasion - with but little success - was interrupted by the Albigensian Crusade. Chapter Three describes the establishment of the Inquisition, its purpose and its method of procedure. Chapter Four comes to grips with the peculiar features of the inquisitorial process: the secrecy of witnesses, the lack of defense lawyers, and the methods of proof, particularly torture. Finally, our survey concludes with a discussion of the penances and penalties: spiritual, pilgrimages, wearing of crosses, confiscations, imprisonment, and the death penalty. A brief Epilogue contrasts the thirteenth century mind with that of the twentieth.

Method of approach. I have already addressed the academic community in *The Popes and Heresy in the Thirteenth Century* (Villanova, Penna.: Augustinian Press, 1949), and in the "The Secrecy of Witnesses in Inquisitorial Tribunals and in Contemporary Criminal Trials," in *Essays in Medieval Life and Thought, Presented in Honor of Austin Patterson Evans* (New York: Columbia University Press, 1955). But these works find a very limited audience along with some 120 books and articles published each year on this topic. They are submerged amid the multiple, disparate and specialized research studies that expand the classic bibliographies on heresy and the Inquisition.

But there is a perennial, if at times perverse, interest in this topic, and the general reading public would, no doubt, appreciate a less formal appraisal of this religious history, one independent of the scholarly apparatus so close (and rightly so) to the heart of the professional historian - the *oeuvre documentée* with its overwhelming footnotes, foreign language citations, and professional jargon. It is for the general reading public that I would like to write a history of the medieval Inquisition. Not that the requisite research has not been done. It has. But the critical apparatus will not be permitted to intrude on the readability of the developing account. Cicero set the standard long ago: the first law of history is not to dare to utter falsehood; the second is not to fear to speak the truth, and moreover no room must be left for suspicion of partiality or prejudice.[5] To this must be added a sympathetic knowledge of the medieval milieu: the ages of faith, the feudal, religious, political, military and social world of the thirteenth century, else an understanding of religious dissidence in that period will forever remain an incomprehensible mystery. G.K. Chesterton in another context made this point with characteristic incisiveness:

> In every case what he knew was a fragmentary fact. In every case what he did not know was the truth behind the fact. What he did not know was the atmosphere. What he did not know was the tradition.[6]

INTRODUCTION

The reception of the first edition of the *Medieval Inquisition* generated very little substantive, negative criticism beyond minor slips and typographical errors. Reviewers generally acknowledged the historical accuracy and precision of the presentation.[1] Objective, balanced scholarship was the guiding principle of the teaching and writing of my Professors Austin Patterson Evans and Lynn Thorndike at Columbia University to whom this volume is dedicated. And that is the way this book was written. Hence there is little reason for revising the current text. The main books utilized in writing this work are included in the bibliography, and two additional bibliographical tools are noted. A list of reviews are appended, and the footnotes have been expanded to include pertinent citations and references.

However some few reviewers took exception from their own personal perceived ideas of how the Medieval Inquisition should be viewed, e.g., Alexander Murray. The late Professor of Medieval History at Cambridge University, Walter Ullmann, among others, had to take note of this bias on a number of occasions:

> It cannot be denied that the knowledge of the principles and the structure of medieval proceedings, both criminal and civil, is somewhat obscured by a mist of prejudice and of consequent ill-informed criticism.[2]

> In hardly any other field of legal history is the prejudice against medieval practice and doctrines more marked than in the domain of criminal procedure. The very words "inquisition," and "torture," and so on, cause painful associations in the modern mind which firmly resists the temptation to obtain reliable data by research into the original sources: these alone can throw some light on contemporary procedural principles . . . And yet, in spite of the prolific output on the part of the medieval professors, the true state of affairs is deplorably blurred by the maze of prejudice which furnishes, one suspects, a welcome justification for the further neglect of relevant medieval writings.[3]

And so once again we are faced with the strong feelings that discussion of the Medieval Inquisition so often engenders - and this by academics who by profession so pride themselves on their dispassionate, objective approach—*wie es eigentlich gewesen ist*. As the *Historiographie du catharisme* so aptly demonstrates, this ideal suffers serious reverses, particularly when religious controversy enters.

This unfortunately being so, it would seem pertinent to review the history of historical writing in regard to the Medieval Inquisition. The recent publication of an entire issue of the renowned *Cahiers de Fanjeaux* on this subject is topical. Professor Henri Maisonneuve of the Catholic Faculties of Lille has indited a magisterial review of this volume, which he has kindly consented to be translated and re-published.[4]

To bring our survey down to the present day a discussion of two major writers of markedly disparate methodologies would seem to be in order. Henry Charles Lea set the tone for much of the opinion of the twentieth century not only in the United States but in Europe as well. Professor Emmanuel Le Roy Ladurie has brought the ideas of the *Annales* school of thought to the marketplace. Thus these three appendices will outline how the Medieval Inquisition has fared at the hands of the historians from the thirteenth through the twentieth century.

ACKNOWLEDGMENTS

With gratitude I wish to acknowledge the kind permission granted me to quote from the following works: Jean Duvernoy, ed., *Le Registre de l'Inquisition de Jacques Fournier, évêque de Pamiers (1318-1325),* (Toulouse: Privat, 1965), 3 vols.; trans. and annot. (New York: Mouton, 1978), 3 vols.; Yves Dossat, *Les Crises de l'Inquisition toulousaine au XIIIe siècle (1233-1273),* (Bordeaux: Imprimerie Bière, 1959); M. l'abbé Henri Maisonneuve, *Études sur les origines de l'Inquisition,* (Paris: J. Vrin, 1960); Walter L. Wakefield and Austin P. Evans, eds. and trans., *Heresies of the High Middle Ages,* (New York: Columbia University Press, 1969); Walter L. Wakefield, *Heresy, Crusade and Inquisition in Southern France, 1100-1250,* (Berkeley: University of California Press, 1975); Rev. Joseph N. Garvin, C.S.C. and James A. Corbett, eds., *The Summa Contra Haereticos, Ascribed to Praepositinus of Cremona,* (University of Notre Dame Press, 1958); Rev. Maurice Bévenot, S.J., "The Inquisition and its Antecedents," *Heythrop Journal,* 7 (1966); Raoul J. van Caenegem, "The Public Prosecution of Crime in Twelfth-Century England," *Church and Government in the Middle Ages,* eds. C.N.L. Brooke and D.E. Luscombe, (Cambridge University Press, 1976).

CHAPTER I
THE CHRISTIAN COMMITMENT OF THE MIDDLE AGES

From the time of Charlemagne (800-814) and beyond, all the peoples of Europe worshipped the one spiritual God according to the teachings and practice of the Roman Church. Christendom comprised a gradually expanding feudal organization of various tribes and ethnic groups in western and central Europe. All professed the same Faith as the common heritage of noble and peasant alike. This unity of Faith and feudal organization was held to be the cornerstone of the stability of society itself. So deep and abiding was this consensus that any deviation from the common faith was felt to be a serious threat to the community itself and hence at times resulted in mob violence.

From time to time individuals rejected the common faith and preached their own brand of religion. Peter of Bruys left his monastery in the early twelfth century and led a group of followers on a preaching mission in southern France. Rejecting the Mass and the Holy Eucharist he condemned churches and altars and forbade the veneration of the cross. Finally, infuriated at this, the populace rose up and hurled him into a fire of burning crosses he had kindled. Similarly, Henry of Lausanne left his Cluniac monastery to denounce the rites and authority of the Roman Church and eventually faded from view. These were isolated episodes, that flamed for the moment and left the scene. These individuals formed no organized sects and their followers dispersed with their death. To the extent that they denied articles of the Catholic Faith they were termed heretics. This term did not apply to Jews, Mohammedans, and pagans who had never accepted Christianity in the first place.

With the second half of the twelfth century, however, there appeared two groups that seriously challenged the basic unity of Christendom. The Albigensians and the Waldensians, particularly in southern France, formed religious sects that denied the basic tenets of the Roman religion, proposed their own creeds and practices, and organized their followers into permanent congregations. This developing religious dissidence was viewed as a dangerous threat to the unity of Christendom. Moreover the very nature of the beliefs and practices of both these heretical sects struck at the roots of the political and social fabric of society itself. So iniquitous were heresies considered to be that the first violent reactions came not from the authorities, ecclesiastical or civil, but from the populace themselves.

What then were the teachings and practices of the Albigensians and the Waldensians? Nothing would seem to be simpler than to list the beliefs of both sects, as it is for those of the Roman Church — but it is not so easy. Neither had a unified structure, although the Albigensians had bishops and deacons, and later on so did the Waldensians. Both were made up of differing groups, often at odds with each other, though maintaining a spiritual community of common ideas. Most of the contemporary information regarding the two sects derives from polemical documents, from treatises composed by defectors, and very little from works by Albigensian and Waldensian adherents themselves. Albigensianism differed from Waldensianism in many ways, for whereas the Waldensians remained fundamentally Christian, the Albigensians absorbed large quantities of oriental myths and rejected the very basics of Christainity, all the while claiming to be "good Christians." While both sects quoted the Bible extensively, they disputed each other's interpretation with unremitting enthusiasm rivaled only by their mutual antagonism to the Roman Church.

1. THE ALBIGENSIANS OR CATHARS

The Albigensians were an admixture of revivalism and eastern myths. They sought to restore the pristine message of the Gospel, while adopting an ancient oriental mythological explanation for the obvious existence of evil in the world. For the Albigensians there were no heroes or saints whose leadership or writings dominated their teachings. Even the names by which they are known lack precision. "Albigensian" derives from the town of Albi in southern France, although it was by no means the most important or the most populous center of their activities. "Cathar" was another name given to this group. It is derived from the Greek word "the pure one" and strictly speaking applied only to the leading class, the "Perfects" or the "Perfected" but commonly it has been ascribed to the sect as a whole. In early years the Perfected wore black clothes to symbolize their rejection of wordly luxury, however in times of persecution, since this distinctive garb served to identify them, they substituted a black thread tied beneath their clothes. Among themselves they were known simply as "good Christians" or as "the good men."

Beliefs of the Albigensians, Cathars.

It has been argued long and learnedly whether Catharism was a native product of western Europe, or whether its dominant myths were imported from eastern Europe — and the resolution is not in sight. However, the influence of Bogomilism, a dualistic sect from Bulgaria attributing all material creation to the devil, seems well founded. As in the case of a number of medieval terms (e.g., feudalism, manorialism, etc.) the description of Catharism must be circumscribed by questions of time (12th or 13th century) and of place (southern France or northern Italy). In a similar context it is well to add that however truthful the Cathars may have tried to be — and that is one of their virtues — logical reasoning suffered repeated, major defeats in their teachings.

The first and most basic belief of the Albigensians or

Cathars was that there are two gods; hence it is dualistic. One god, the good god in heaven, is spiritual and created all spiritual beings including man's soul. The other god is evil, and he created all material things, including the world and all that is in it, particularly man except for his soul. Various myths were evolved to explain the perennial problem of the existence of evil in the world. One version held that satan, the devil, was originally a good angel or son of god who fell and then created the visible world, all of which is evil like himself. This is known as mitigated dualism, since the good god was still supreme. Another version said that there were two eternal, all-powerful principles, the good god and the bad god, the god of light and the god of darkness, who persist in eternal, irreducible opposition. This is absolute dualism. These two opinions were argued out between two factions of the Cathars in northern Italy at the time. In the *Book of the Two Principles*[1], written by a Cathar, one faction posed the question: how could the good god create angels who would fall, for then he would be the cause of evil, which is obviously impossible? Therefore there must be two all-powerful gods, two first principles. To this the moderate dualists replied in summary that such a position deprived angels (and consequently men, for men's souls were said to be the fallen angels) of free will, the opportunity for doing good, and indeed denied personal responsibility for one's acts. This denial of free will would thus be fatal to all society! In any case it was absolute dualism that prevailed after the visit of a missionary named Nicetas from Constantinople. At an organizational and doctrinal assembly of the Cathars in Languedoc at St. Felix-de-Caraman (ca. 1167-1172) Nicetas convinced the assembly of the necessity for the belief of two eternal principles.[2]

To accommodate each belief, various myths were circulated. The god of the Old Testament created the world, which is evil; hence the Old Testament was repudiated. The New Testament, as interpreted by the Cathars, was followed rigidly as the guide to the true apostolic life. The problem of life, put very simply, was for man to free his spiritual soul, which was good, from his body, which was evil. The soul had been created good by the good god, but had rebelled and was imprisoned by the devil in a material body. Man atones for his crimes by enduring the vicissitudes of life, divesting himself of all material attachments, and at death returns to his original home, heaven. Since the process of purgation may not be successfully completed in one lifetime, by a process of reincarnation, the soul may have to pass through a number of other bodies, including animals. One Cathar recalled that he had previously been a horse and had lost a shoe in the locality; and sure enough, as he passed by the place, there it was.[3] Cleansing from all sin could be obtained only through the reception of the *consolamentum*, a ritual ceremony that wiped out all sin and imparted the holy spirit (a creature inferior to the son of god, Christ) who was head of the angels guarding men's souls. Thus purgatory, the place where souls were purified after death from the remaining effects of sin, was denied, and metempsychosis adopted, wherein souls were purged by repeated reincarnations. For this reason, too, the Albigensians rejected the Sacrament of Penance, the Mass, and prayers for the dead.

It was to teach this way to salvation, the reception of the *consolamentum*, that the good god sent his son, Christ, into the world. Christ, according to the Cathars, was not god, but was an angel, who did not have a body since he had not sinned. Hence, Christ only had the appearance of a body, a mirage. Mary, therefore, could not have borne him, since he was an angel. Thus the Holy Trinity was denied since both the holy spirit and Christ, according to the Cathars, were created angels, not god. Further, Christ could not have suffered and died on the cross, or risen from the dead — these were only illusions! Christ's mission on earth was not to redeem mankind by his suffering and death on the cross, but rather to instruct man how to liberate his soul from sin by the reception of the *consolamentum.* Hence there would be no resurrection of the body. Devotions to the crucifix and to the saints were a mockery. Church buildings were quite useless since one could worship god in a stable quite as well as in a church, where god does not live.

The moral code of the Cathars was dominated by two beliefs:

1) that all material things were evil and were to be avoided at all costs; 2) the moral teachings of Christ were to be followed minutely. A contemporary authority, Rainier Sacconi, a convert from Catharism, summarized their teachings thus:

> The general beliefs of all the Cathars are as follows: The devil made this world and everything in it. Also, that all the sacraments of the Church, namely baptism of actual water and the other sacraments, are of no avail for salvation and that they are not the true sacraments of Christ and His Church but are deceptive and diabolical and belong to the church of the wicked ... Also a common belief to all Cathars is that carnal matrimony has always been a mortal sin and that in the future life one incurs no heavier a penalty for adultery or incest than for legitimate marriage, nor indeed among them should anyone be more severely punished on this account. Also, Cathars deny the future resurrection of the body. Also, they believe that to eat meat, eggs, or cheese, even in pressing need, is a mortal sin; this for the reason that they are begotten by coition. Also that taking an oath is in no case permissible,

> this consequently, is a mortal sin. Also, that secular authorities commit mortal sin in punishing malefactors or heretics. Also, that no one can attain salvation except in their sect. Also, that all children, even the baptized, will endure no lighter punishments in eternity than will thieves and murderers.[4]

Intimately bound up with proper living was the organization developed by the Cathars, for this was a very austere way of life and had to be adapted to the frailties of nature. There were two classes of Cathars: the Perfected, and the *credentes*, the believers. Only the Perfected were required to observe the moral code in all its rigor. A candidate prepared himself for admission to this order by an extended period of rigorous trial, abstinence and instruction. He was expected to know thoroughly the doctrines of Catharism, to be able to teach them effectively and to defend them with his life. After at least a full year of living the life of the Perfected in all its strictness and mortification the initiate received the *consolamentum* in a two part ceremony. First, he was empowered to recite "the Lord's Prayer" with full understanding — no layman was permitted to say it. Second, after a sermon explaining the Cathar doctrine, the candidate requested baptism which was imposed by the laying on of hands by a Perfected while the book of the Gospels was held over his head.

A contemporary Provencal ritual, 1250-1280, describes the ceremony as follows:

> Let the elder take the Book and place it on the believer's head, and the other Good Men place each his right hand on him. Then let them say the Pardon [a formula spoken by the leaders and the congregation asking forgiveness for their sins] and the "Let us adore" [the father, the son and the holy

spirit] thrice, and then, 'Holy Father, receive Thy servant in Thy righteousness and bestow Thy grace and Thy Holy Spirit upon him.

Then let them pray to God with the Prayer [the Our Father] and let him who conducts the service say the Six [repetition of the Lord's Prayer six times] in a low voice. When the Six is finished, let him say 'Let us adore' thrice, the Prayer once in full voice, and then the Gospel. When the Gospel has been read, let them say 'Let us adore' thrice, the Grace [May the Grace of our Lord Jesus Christ be with you all] and the Pardon. Then they should perform the Act of Peace [men embraced each other with a kiss on each cheek]. Let woman believers, if there are any present, perform the Act of Peace with the Book and with each other. And then let them pray to God with a Double [sixteen repetitions of the Our Father], with obeisances. And thus they will have administered [the consolamentum].[5]

This ritual in a loose sense might be compared with the sacraments of baptism, confirmation, extreme unction, and ordination: baptism, not by water which was material and therefore evil, but by the imposition of hands, whereby sin was forgiven. According to the Cathars reception of the *consolamentum* was the only way that sins could be removed and it could be administered only once in a lifetime. It resembled Confirmation, for the holy spirit, the guardian of souls, was thereby implanted. This rite was compared with Extreme Unction, for the soul was now liberated from all attachment to material things and was prepared to return to heaven. Finally, it was likened to Ordination, for now the initiate was Perfected and could administer the rite to others and could teach all the doctrines of the Cathars. In this regard one must note that it was of first importance that the conferring Perfected be himself without sin at the moment of the imposition of hands — and remain so in the future — otherwise the *consolamentum* so conferred was invalid and worthless, and as a result the candidate remained in sin and could not be saved. This teaching was a cause of great anxiety, for one could never be certain that the conferring Perfected was without sin. In fact, when some Perfected changed doctrine (e.g., at the meeting at St. Felix-de-Caraman when the basic change was made from mitigated to absolute dualism) many Perfected had to be "reconsoled." Similarly, if the ordaining Perfected sinned, as some of them did with women, then all those previously "consoled" by him immediately lost their innocence. Also, if after having been "consoled" the Perfected himself committed sin, the situation was equally serious since the *consolamentum* was supposed to be given only once. The severity of this teaching becomes more meaningful in view of the anti-sacerdotal attitude (the denial of the Divine power of the Sacrament of Holy Orders and the necessity of the priesthood) of both the Cathars and the Waldensians. According to them the effectiveness of the rite depends upon the sanctity of the conferring minister. Hence, they held that unworthy priests could not validly administer the sacraments. In contrast, the Roman Church held and holds that the validity of the sacraments depends upon the legitimate ordination of the priest and not on his current spiritual condition.

Once a person, man or woman, had been "consoled" he was solemnly committed for the rest of his life to a most austere regime of rigid observances. All sins of the flesh, including thoughts, were totally forbidden. In addition to never eating meat, eggs, milk, or cheese, he was required to fast three days each week, Monday, Wednesday and Friday, on bread and water. Moreover they observed three forty-day fasts during the year: during Lent, from

Pentecost to the feast of Saint Peter, and the third, from the feast of St. Martin until Christmas. Absolute celibacy was mandatory. All killing of animals was forbidden, for one could never be sure that the animal was not carrying the spirit of a man who had not yet been "consoled." The new Perfected was invested with a distinctive black clothing (one immediately thinks of the black clerical garb worn by Catholic priests today). Since such austerity of life was possible only for the chosen few, the *consolamentum* was usually reserved for the vast majority until the end of life. Death was looked upon as a good since the soul would then be liberated from the prison of the evil flesh. The problem was that it was not always easy to determine whether the sick person was actually going to die or not. Moreover the person to be "consoled" had to be conscious in order to be able to recite the Lord's Prayer, otherwise he was not permitted to receive the *consolamentum*. Consequently, when a person neared death, he received the *consolamentum*. However if he showed signs of recovery and would have to undertake the almost impossible burdens of the Perfected with the possibility of moral relapse, death could be laudably hastened by the practice called the *endura*. This meant in most cases that all food was withheld from the dying person so that he expired from starvation. The *endura* was available not only to the mortally ill, but also to Cathars in prison to enable them to forestall going to the stake, and to children, who ordinarily were not admitted to the *consolamentum*.[6] Just how often this rite was used is impossible to ascertain.

The actual structure of the Cathar church was somewhat informal. It was organized into dioceses with the bishop elected from among the local Perfected. He enjoyed a primacy among equals, the other Perfected. In his work he was assisted by an 'elder son' and a 'younger son', a distinction having nothing to do with age but with the order of succession. It was their prime duty to preach, to 'console' and to preside at the other Catharist rites. Deacons maintained hospices for traveling Perfected and for the training of candidates for the reception of the *consolamentum.*

The other class of the Cathars were the *credentes*, the 'believers.' These followers believed in and supported the Perfected, but did not themselves undertake their stringent obligations. The 'believer' lived in the world, was free to marry, to engage in commerce, to take up arms, to accumulate wealth, and to eat whatever he desired. There was no Cathar moral code for the 'believer.' He entered the sect through the rite called the *convenientia*, which was a solemn commitment to receive the *consolamentum* before death and was conferred by the imposition of hands. Other ritual observances of the Cathars were the *melioramentum*, a form of 'veneration' of the Perfected by Believers, who upon meeting them would genuflect three times and request a blessing that they might receive the *consolamentum* before they died. The Perfected would reply: "May God be prayed that he make you a good Christian," which meant to them becoming a Cathar. The *apparellamentum* or *servitium* was a monthly public confession of minor faults, for the Perfected had no mortal sins. It was apparently a ritual formula, strongly reminiscent of the *Confiteor* recited at a Catholic Mass by the celebrant and the congregation. Since all violations of the Cathar moral code were equally serious and mortal, e.g., drinking milk, taking an oath, stealing, murder, this Service was not valid for the remitting of such sins, since the *consolamentum* itself was the only means for forgiving sins. All the above sins entailed the immediate loss of the *consolamentum* and plunged the delinquent once more into the devil's domain, the material world.

A 'blessing of bread' before the regular meal was made by a Perfected, who said the Lord's Prayer, broke the bread into pieces and gave it to his assistants to distribute, saying: "The grace of the Lord be with you." This blessed bread was by no means considered to be the Body and Blood of Christ. The main and really the only prayer of the Cathars was the Lord's Prayer. It could be recited only by those who had been 'consoled' and they recited it many times a day. The Provençal ritual was quite definite on this subject: "The office ... of saying the Prayer should not be confided to a layman."

Biblical proofs for their beliefs adduced by the Cathars.

Most of the dissident religious sects of western Europe were evangelical; they supported their beliefs by citations from the Bible. Characteristically they were highly selective in their use of biblical passages, and often their exegesis, explanation of the chosen text, was even more bizarre. This was especially true of the Cathars. Following one of the treatises written towards the end of the twelfth century in France one may ascertain the mode of reasoning adopted by the Albigensians.[7]

After stating the basic tenet of Catharism, that there are two gods, the good god who created spiritual beings which are good, and the bad god, the devil, who created material things which are bad, the author proceeds to adduce the biblical proofs for each of their beliefs and the reasoning whereby they arrived at such a conclusion.

The bad god created the world and all material things, including man's body.

Biblical proof: In Genesis III,22, it is said: "Adam has become like one of us." This was said after Adam had become nothing other than a sinner. Hence it appears that it is precisely as a sinner that Adam is like the one who spoke thus. Therefore he who spoke thus was a sinner and was not the Omnipotent God. But the god who thus spoke had created heaven and earth and all visible things. The Omnipotent God, therefore, did not create visible things; hence it follows that the devil did. The Albigensians thus concluded that the creator of the world and all material things, including man's body, is the god of darkness, the bad god, Satan.

Commenting in like fashion on Genesis VI,5-7: "When the Lord saw that man had done much evil on earth and that his thoughts and inclinations were always evil," and Genesis VIII,21: "The senses of man and the thoughts of the human heart from youth are prone to evil," the Cathars noted that god repented that he had created man: Genesis VI,7: "He was sorry that he had made man." From these quotations the Cathars reasoned that if man from his very youth was prone to evil, this proclivity had to be part of his nature. If then this evil tendency was part of man's nature it had to be due to his body or his soul. It could not be due to his soul which had been made to the image and likeness of God, therefore it had to be according to his body. Hence corporeal nature is evil and could not have been created by the Omnipotent God; therefore the devil did. The conclusion is inescapable: man except for his soul was created by the devil.

Man does not have a free will. Man cannot perform a good act. Biblical proof: Jeremiah XIII,23: "Can the Nubian change his skin, or the leopard its spots? And you? Can you do good, you who are schooled in evil?" Obviously, the Cathars reasoned, the first is impossible; therefore man is evil by nature and cannot do good; he has no free will. Father Marie-Humbert Vicaire[8] states the Cathar position baldly when he writes that for them there is no sin because there is no free will; a person is good or bad by nature. This conclusion was deduced by the Cathars from Matthew VII, 17-18: "A good tree always yields good fruit, and a bad tree bad fruit. A good tree cannot bear bad fruit, or a bad tree good fruit."

In a similar fashion the Albigensians argued that: *Man is contrary to God.* Proof: Job VII,20 "O watcher of men, why have you placed me contrary to you?"

Man comes from the devil. Proof: John VIII,44: "Your father is the devil." and I John III,8: "The man who sins is a child of the devil."

The devil is called prince of this world. Proof: By Christ in John XII,31; XVI,11 and by St. Paul in Ephesians II,1-2: "Time was when you were dead in your sins and wickedness, when you followed the evil ways of this present age, when you obeyed the commander of the spiritual powers of the air, the spirit now at work among God's real subjects."

Man's body and soul are in conflict. Proof: St. Paul in Romans VII,23 says: "I perceive that there is in my bodily members a different law, fighting against the law that my reason approves and making me a prisoner under the law that is in my members, the law of sin." Romans VII,24: "Miserable creature that I am, who is there to rescue me out of this body doomed to death."

Cathars rejected the Old Testament. The Albigensians contended that the Old Testament was given to man, not by Almighty God, but by the god of darkness, and that no one was saved before Christ came on earth.

Scriptural proof: The god of the Old Testament gave precepts that were not good: Ezekiel XX,25: "I imposed on them statutes that were not good statutes, and laws by which they could not win life." These words apply to the commandments of the Old Testament, the Cathars pointed out. The precepts of the Old Testament are, therefore, not good, and are not maxims of life. Hence they are evil and could not have been given by God Almighty, but only by the devil, the god of the Old Testament.

The god of the Old Testament and the God of the New Testament are different gods. Scriptural proof:

The god of the O.T. called himself a killer and a punisher: Deuteronomy XXXII,39: "I put to death ... I smite." On the other hand the God of the N.T. preached gentleness and forgiveness: Matthew XI,29: "Learn of me, for I am gentle and humble-hearted." Again, according to the Old Law we are to hate our enemies; the New Law forbids it: Matthew V,43: "You have learned that they were told, 'Love your neighbor, hate your enemy,' but what I tell you is this: Love your enemies." Therefore from these citations the Cathars concluded that the god of the Old Testament and the God of the New Testament cannot be the same.

Salvation came only with the New Law. Biblical proof: Matthew XI,12: "Ever since the coming of John the Baptist the kingdom of heaven has been subjected to violence, and the violent bear it away." Hence it was only from the time of the Baptist that men afflicted themselves on account of the kingdom of heaven and thus began to merit heaven. Therefore, before this time men did not merit heaven and hence were not saved.

John the Baptist himself lacked faith and therefore was not saved. Scriptural proof:

Matthew XI,2-3: "John, who was in prison, heard what Christ was doing, and sent his own disciples to him with this message: 'Are you the one who is to come, or are we to expect some other?" From this the Cathars reasoned that John doubted Christ, did not believe in him, hence lacked faith and could not please God, for, according to Hebrews XI,6: "Without faith it is impossible for anyone to please God." Therefore, the Albigensians concluded, John was evil and was damned.

Christ had no human body. The Cathars taught that Christ had no human flesh, did not suffer and die, did not rise from the dead, and that consequently there will be no final resurrection of the human body. Scriptural proof:

Matthew I,18: "When Mary the mother of Jesus was engaged to Joseph, but before they lived together she was found to be with child by the Holy Spirit." "Notice," the Cathars argued, "that it said 'by the Spirit' and not 'by the flesh.' But in John III,6: Christ said: "what is born of flesh is flesh and what is born of spirit is spirit." Therefore, the Cathars, reasoned, Christ was a spirit and not a material being. This fact is further substantiated in Matthew I,20: "Joseph, son of David." said the angel, "do not be afraid to take Mary home with

> you as your wife. For what has been conceived within her is of the Holy Spirit." 'Within her,' not 'of her' it says. Obviously Christ was spiritual and had no material body.
>
> Consequently Mary was not his mother. Jesus himself made this clear: "Someone came to him saying 'Your mother and your brothers are outside looking for you.' But Jesus said 'Who is my mother? Who are my brothers?' And extending his hands towards his disciples, he added: 'Here are my mother and my brothers. Whoever does the will of my heavenly Father is my brother, my sister, my mother." Matthew XII,49-50.
>
> Another sign that Christ did not have a body, the Cathars claimed, was the fact that he walked on water, whereas Peter, who was in the flesh, tried to do so and sank: Matthew XIV,28-30: "Peter spoke up and said: 'Lord, if it is really you, tell me to come to you across the water.' 'Come,' he said. So Peter got out of the boat and began to walk on the water, moving toward Jesus. But when he perceived how strong the wind was, becoming frightened, he began to sink and cried out, 'Lord save me!' Jesus at once stretched out his hand and caught him."

Marriage is evil. The Cathars taught that no one could be saved in marriage, citing Christ's words: Matthew XIX,12: "There are others who have themselves renounced marriage for the sake of the kingdom of heaven. Let those accept it who can." In support of this interpretation they quoted Saint Augustine and also Saint Paul: I Corinthians VII,29: " The time we live in will not last long. While it lasts men should be as if they had no wives." In this same context Christ expressed pity for the pregnant and for nursing mothers: Matthew XXIV,19: "Alas for women with child in those days, and for those who have children at the breast!" The words 'alas for the pregnant' was interpreted by the Cathars as meaning it was evil to be pregnant, that the child of the pregnancy was evil, that all coition was evil, and that therefore one must abstain from marital intercourse. Further, Christ stated that those worthy of resurrection would not marry: Luke XX,34-35: "The men and women of this world marry: but those who have been judged worthy of a place in the other world and of the resurrection from the dead, do not marry."

The eating of meat is forbidden. Scriptural proof:

The Albigensians cited Saint Jerome as stating that the first inhabitants of the earth did not eat meat, and further that Saint Paul forbade it: Romans XIV,21: "It is good not to eat meat or drink wine." They noted the fact, too, that Christ gave the crowds fish and bread to eat several times and ate them himself, but we never read of him eating meat. Therefore meat is prohibited.

Sin. The doctrine of the Albigensians on sin is particularly obscure; for on the one hand they denied that man had free will, which is an essential prerequisite for committing sin. On the other hand they did speak about sin, enumerated a large number of them (all dietary breaches being mortal), and had their own ritual, the *service*, for confessing minor faults. This ceremony did not apply to major offenses since mortal sins could only be removed by the reception of the *consolamentum* which could only be given once.

All the good will gain the same reward; all the wicked will receive the same punishment.

According to the Albigensians, punishments and rewards, sins and good deeds were of equal depravity or merit. No wicked person was worse than another; no good person better than another.

Biblical proof: In substantiation for this anomaly the Cathars adduced the parable of the weeds: Matthew XIII,40-42: "As the darnel, then, is gathered up and burnt, so at the end of time the Son of Man will send out his angels, who will gather out of his kingdom whatever makes men stumble, and all whose deeds are evil, and these will be thrown into the blazing furnace, the place of wailing and grinding of teeth." The Cathars reasoned that the punishments were common to all the wicked — fire, tears, and grinding teeth — hence all the wicked received equal punishment. By similar process of deduction they concluded that all the good will obtain the same reward, just as the workers in the vineyard, no matter how long they worked, all received the same pay (Matthew XX,9-10). Similar conclusions were drawn from the parable of the guest without a wedding garment — signifying all the wicked (Matthew XXII, 2-13) — and the eternal fire provided for all the damned (Matthew XXV,41) — the same fire for all the damned regardless of the nature or the number of their crimes. In like manner the just will shine as the sun (Matthew XIII,43); hence all equally. So too, eternal life is the knowledge of God, but, as the Cathars pointed out, everyone will know God as He is (John XVII,3; I Corinthians XIII,12); therefore all the saved will enjoy an equal reward.

In summary, these are the doctrines and practices of the Cathars; what they believed, what they taught, and why.

2. THE BELIEFS AND PRACTICES OF THE WALDENSIANS

The other main group of religious dissidents of the high Middle Ages was that of the followers of Valdès of Lyons.

Fundamentally evangelical, the Waldensians sought to teach the pristine message of the Gospel and to live in absolute poverty. There was certainly nothing heretical about that. They were Christians and always remained so. The clearest introduction to the Waldensians is to recapitulate the few details that are known about its founder. His name is spelt a number of different ways in the documents, but there is absolutely no foundation for giving him the name 'Peter' which traditionally has been added to his name.

Valdès appears to have been a rich merchant of Lyons, in the 1170's, who chanced one day to hear a jongleur on a street chant the song of Saint Alexis. According to the legend, Alexis was a wealthy young man who, on the day of his wedding, left his bride, renounced his wealth, and departed to a distant town to live in poverty, eventually returning to die, unrecognized as a servant, in his former home. Profoundly moved, Valdès inquired from a master of theology: "What is the surest way to go to God?" Citing the evangelical counsel of perfection Christ gave to the rich young man in the Gospel, the theologian replied: "If you wish to go the whole way, go, sell your possessions, and give to the poor, and then you will have riches in heaven, and come follow me." (Matthew XIX,21) And that is precisely what Valdès did.

He returned home, made appropriate arrangments for his wife and two daughters, sold the rest of his possesions, and went into the streets to beg his living. Since he did not read Latin, Valdès requested a young scribe to write while a grammarian translated and dictated, the New Testament, the Psalter (150 psalms) and some writings of the Church Fathers into the vernacular, "occitan," the patois of the Midi. These he memorized — which was the way his followers learned the Scriptures — and began preaching in the streets. His basic commitment was to teach to the ordinary person Christ's message as contained in the

Gospel, and to live according to it in voluntary, absolute poverty. His obvious sincerity soon attracted a following of both men and women, for the most part illiterate, who joined him preaching in the streets, public places, and even in churches. Difficulties seem to have arisen precisely in regard to their two main virtues, preaching and poverty. On the one hand, they were of the laity without training in Scripture or theology, and were therefore unprepared, according to the local bishop, to preach. On the other hand, their insistence on absolute poverty brought into question the devotion of the clergy who did not adopt this rigorous way of life. Encountering displeasure from ecclesiastical authorities on account of his unauthorized preaching, Valdès apparently took his cause to Rome. There we encounter diverse accounts from the chroniclers.[9] One, Walter Map, an Englishman, said that the pope appointed a commission to examine Valdès which laughed him out of court; another, the Chronicle of Laon, stated that Pope Alexander III received him kindly, approved his life of poverty, and admonished him not to preach without the local bishop's permission. The occitan translation of the New Testament which Valdès presented to the Pope for approval at this time was undoubtedly ratified.[10]

Back in Lyons, Valdès made a Profession of Faith[11] before a diocesan synod, 1180/81. This document covered a wide variety of Catholic doctrine which Valdès had no difficulty in accepting. However shortly thereafter the new archbishop of Lyons forbade Valdès to preach. He, in turn, declined to obey on the biblical ground given by St. Peter to the High Priest in Jerusalem: "We must obey God rather than man" (Acts V,29) and the mandate of Christ Himself: "Go forth to every part of the world, and proclaim the Good News to the whole creation." (Mark XVI,15) It has been suggested that the novel introduction of women as preachers may have been the proximate cause hastening episcopal disapproval. Here it was basically a question of disobedience, and because Valdès contumaciously refused to obey, the archbishop excommunicated him and expelled him from the city. He and his followers left the city, travelling to the Midi and also over the Alps, and eventually split into two major divisions, the Poor of Lyons in southern France and the Poor Lombards in northern Italy. Not being theologically or scripturally knowledgeable and drifting farther away from central authority, they began to adopt some of the doctrines of other sects and were formally condemned at Verona in 1184 by the decree *Ad abolendam.*

Of the final years of Valdès himself little is known, even the time and place of his death are mere conjectures. His ideas were quite definite: preach the Gospel, refrain from any church structure or form of organization that would inhibit preaching, and practice absolute poverty. Under the gentle direction of Pope Innocent III two groups of the Waldensians did return to the Roman Church, as it seems Valdès himself intended to do: one section under the leadership of Durand of Huesca in 1208; another under the direction of Bernard Prim in 1210 in Lombardy.

Unlike the Cathars, the Waldensians had neither the will nor the intention of developing a full scale speculative theology. As Herbert Grundmann, President of the *Monumenta Germaniae Historica* has well said, it was neither popular nor social, in the ordinary meaning of those terms. Indeed they stood apart from the society of that time without ever becomming revolutionary, aggressive or subversive. They were, in a word, religious, Christian, biblical. In their early debates with the Cathars they maintained basically the Christian position.

Three periods may be distinguished in the early history of the Waldensians: from its beginning up to about 1207 when Valdès himself maintained a commanding leadership; secondly, from the debate at Pamiers in 1207 to the general meeting at Bergamo in 1218; and thirdly their separate ways thereafter. Valdès himself strongly held to his total commitment to preaching the Gospel, and to living a life of absolute poverty. Towards preserving these two fundamental principles he opposed every attempt to construct a hierarchy, a church structure. His moral leadership was sufficient for all their needs. With the public debate at Pamiers in 1207 between the Catholics and the Waldensians a major turning point appears to have occurred. Perhaps Valdès himself was already dead. There is no extant records of the exchange of views, but as a result a number of Waldensians expressed a desire to rejoin the Roman Church, and did so as noted above. On the other hand at about this time, 1205, another group under the leadership of John of Ronco broke away from the French and went their separate way as the 'Poor Lombards.'

In 1218 a general meeting was called at Bergamo in Italy in a serious attempt to iron out the differences between the Poor of Lyons and the Poor Lombards. On a number of questions there was mutual agreement:[12]

- on the election of officials for specific terms of office. Valdès had opposed this.

- on the establishment of the special order of the fully prepared and committed preachers, who alone were entitled to the name 'The Poor,' who wore a particular type of sandals, and were ordained by the imposition of hands by a bishop or other ministers. 'The Poor' of the Waldensians corresponded to the 'Perfected' of the Cathars.

- on the proposition that the Roman Church is not 'the church of God' or the 'church of Christ' but is an evil church from the day that Pope Sylvester accepted possessions for the church.

— in denying that the Roman Church had the power of the keys to remit sin (the Sacrament of Penance), since God alone is capable of forgiving sin.

— on rejection of the teachings of the Roman Church in regard to fasting, indulgences, pilgrimages, visits to the shrines of saints, and prohibition of marriage within certain degrees of kindred.

— on opposition to the building of churches and altars, and the rejection of veneration of the crucifix.

— in denying the existence of purgatory; in rejecting prayers and Masses for the dead; on refusal to take an oath for any reason whatever; in denying the right of civil rulers to punish.

At the same time the Poor of Lyons disagreed with the Poor Lombards on the following issues:

— The Poor of Lyons taught that sacraments administered by a priest were valid regardless of his spiritual condition, while the Lombards held that the sacrament was valueless if the priest was in sin.

— the Poor of Lyons claimed every good person was a priest and the church, but the Lombards argued that the church did not exist unless two assembled together.

— for the Poor of Lyons all work was absolutely forbidden; preaching was their sole occupation. For the Lombards, the 'sandal-wearers' could work.

— over the presence of Christ's Body and Blood in the Eucharist, and on whether a layman could consecrate.

— Against the teaching of Valdès himself, both groups permitted the dissolution of marriage by mutual agreement in order to become 'a Poor,' but the Lombards felt the community should have the right to make the decision.

Eventually the differences between them loomed larger then their points of agreement. The two groups never healed their rift and they both went their separate ways, the Poor of Lyons remaining more moderate, the Lombards much more radical. By the same token both became increasingly anti-clerical and antagonistic to the Roman Church.

Waldensian community. The Waldensians employed a simple, functional organization, although at a later date they adopted the division of bishops, priests and deacons without much differentiation of function among them. After a period of training covering a number of years in which memorization of the Bible held pride of place, the candidate, man or woman, was granted the title of 'Poor,' properly so-called, and given the privilege of wearing their special type of sandal. The wearing of these sandals, 'sandal-shod' was a distinguishing mark of the full-fledged 'Poor,' much as the black garb of the Cathars identified their 'Perfected.' Having renounced all possessions and marriage, the 'Poor' did not engage in any other labor but preaching, calling to repentance, denouncing all sin, and quoting the New Testament at length. Other Waldensians retained their ordinary way of life, supported the preachers, maintained training schools, and attended bible studies in the vernacular, learning great passages by heart. Like their perennial opponents, the Cathars, their main prayer was the 'Our Father." However, they both agreed in rejecting the Roman Church.

Biblical proofs for their teachings. Like the Cathars, the Waldensians based their doctrine on the New Testament. Indeed they frequently disputed with them on many points, demonstrating how the Cathars mistranslated the Scriptures for their own purposes and showing how precious little the Cathars really knew of Holy Writ. Again, too, since the Waldensians remained fundamentally Christian they did not feel it necessary or desirable to concoct a whole new system about the nature of God and His relationship to man. The necessity of preaching the Gospel and the identification of absolute poverty with perfection were the cornerstones of this sect. Where they differed with the Roman Church, they stated their position together with a scripture quotation or two by way of proof without offering further logical deductions or syllogistic reasoning to indicate how they arrived at such a conclusion. Some of their distinctive tenets were:

> *All oaths are prohibited, in court or out of it, without exception*: Matthew V,34-36: "What I tell you is: do not swear at all. Do not swear by heaven (it is God's throne), not by the earth (it is his footstool), nor by Jerusalem (it is the city of the great King); do not swear by your head (you cannot make a single hair white or black)."
>
> *There must be no lying.* Matthew V,37: "Plain 'Yes' or 'No' is all you need to say; anything beyond that comes from the devil."
>
> *Condemned military service*: Matthew XXVI,52: "Put up your sword. All who take the sword die by the sword."
>
> *Any judicial process is forbidden by God and is a sin; it is contrary to God's command for any judge in any case for any reason to sentence a man to corporal punishment involving bloodshed, or to death*: Matthew VII,1; "Pass no judgement, and you will not be judged." Matthew V,21: "You have learned that our forefathers were told, 'Do not commit murder; anyone who commits murder must be brought to judgement.'"

Prayers and Masses for the dead are valueless. John XII,35: "The light is among you still, but not for long. Go on your way while you have the light, so that darkness may not overtake you." II Corinthians V,10: "For we must all have our eyes laid open before the tribunal of Christ, where each must receive what is due him for his conduct in the body, good or bad." II Corinthians VI,2: "In the hour of my favour I gave heed to you; on the day of deliverance I came to your aid." Galatians VI,10: "Therefore, as opportunity offers, let us work for the good of all, especially members of the household of the faith." From these citations the Waldensians argued that each person ought to be responsible for his own salvation, and was not to depend on others to cleanse him before God; this was a personal relationship. Man's destiny was sealed when he died and nothing could change it. Hence there was no purgatory, no need for prayers and Masses for the dead.

All laymen, including women, have the right to preach. James IV, 17: "The man who knows the good he ought to do and does not do it is a sinner." Revelations XXII, 17: 'Come!' say the Spirit and the bride, 'Come' let each hearer reply. Come forward you who are thirsty; accept the water of life, a free gift to all who desire it." Mark IX,39: "Do not stop him; no one who does a work of divine power in my name will be able the next moment to speak evil of me." Titus II,3: "The older women ... must set a high standard, and school the younger women to be loving wives and mothers." Speaking of Anna, the daughter of Phanuel, Luke says: "Coming up at that very moment she returned thanks to God; and she talked about the child to all who were looking for the liberation of Jerusalem." Luke II,38.

> *Reverence should not be given to the Cross or to the Altar.*
>
> "Their idols are silver and gold, made by the hands of men." Psalm CXV,4.

Rejected the authority of the Roman Curch. All the canons and decrees of the Roman Church are merely the traditions of the Pharisees: Matthew XV,3: "Why do you transgress the command of God by your own traditions?"

3. ROMAN CATHOLICISM

The Pope and the General Councils speak for the Catholic Church and no other group or individual has any authority to define or derogate Catholic doctrine. In outlining the main tenets of Catholicism, particularly in relation to the Albigensians and the Waldensians, a number of documents might be cited, e.g., the Profession of Faith by Valdès himself, or the Profession of Faith of Durand of Huesca and his companions quoted by Pope Innocent III in formally establishing their Society of Poor Catholics, but perhaps the most authoritative Catholic teaching contemporary with these events is the first canon of the Fourth Lateran Council 1215.

> *Canon 1* We firmly believe and openly confess that there is only one true God, eternal and immense, omnipotent, unchangeable, incomprehensible, and ineffable, Father, Son, and Holy Spirit; three Persons indeed but one essence, substance, or nature absolutely simple; the Father (proceeding) from no one, but the Son from the Father only, and the Holy Spirit equally from both, always without beginning and end. The Father begetting, the Son begotten, and the Holy Spirit proceeding; consubstantial and co-equal, co-omnipotent and co-eternal, the one principle of the universe, Creator of all things invisible and visible, spiritual

and corporeal, who from the beginning of time and by His omnipotent power made from nothing creatures both spiritual and corporeal, angelic, namely, and mundane, and then human, as it were, common, composed of spirit and body. The devil and the other demons were indeed created by God good by nature but they became bad through themselves; man, however, sinned at the suggestion of the devil. This Holy Trinity in its common essence undivided and in personal properties divided, through Moses, the holy prophets, and other servants gave to the human race at the most opportune intervals of time the doctrine of salvation.

And, finally, Jesus Christ, the only begotten Son of God made flesh by the entire Trinity, conceived with the co-operation of the Holy Spirit of Mary ever Virgin, made true man, composed of a rational soul and human flesh, one Person in two natures, pointed out more clearly the way of life. Who according to His divinity is immortal and impassible, according to His humanity was made passible and mortal, suffered on the cross for the salvation of the human race, and being dead descended into hell, rose from the dead, and ascended into heaven. But He descended in soul, arose in flesh, and ascended equally in both; He will come again at the end of the world to judge the living and the dead and will render to the reprobate and to the elect according to their works, who all shall arise with their own bodies which they now have that they may receive according to their merits, whether good or bad, the latter eternal punishment with the devil, the former eternal glory with Christ.

There is one Universal Church of the faithful, outside of which there is absolutely no salvation. In which there is the same priest and sacrifice, Jesus

> Christ, whose body and blood are truly contained in the sacrament of the altar under the forms of bread and wine; the bread being changed *(transsubstantiatis)* by divine power into the body, and the wine into the blood, so that to realize the mystery of unity we may receive of Him what He has received of us. And this sacrament no one can effect except the priest who has been duly ordained in accordance with the keys of the Church, which Jesus Christ Himself gave to the Apostles and their successors.
>
> But the sacrament of baptism, which by the invocation of each Person of the Trinity, namely, of the Father, Son, and Holy Spirit, is effected in water, duly conferred on children and adults in the form prescribed by the Church by anyone whatsoever, leads to salvation. And should anyone after the reception of baptism have fallen into serious sin, by true repentance he can always be restored. Not only virgins and those practicing chastity, but also those united in marriage, through the right faith and through works pleasing to God, can merit eternal salvation.[13]

Permission to preach within a diocese pertained in the twelfth century as it does in the twentieth to the jurisdiction of the local bishop.

Sacred Scripture being an essential part of the teaching of the Roman Church, required then, as it does now, study and acquired expertise. St. Augustine[14] in the fifth century proclaimed the authority of three rules of Faith: Scripture, Tradition, and the teaching power of the Church. Above the Bible and Tradition is the living authority of the Church, for as Augustine states: "I would not believe in the Gospel unless the authority of the Catholic Church ordered it." It is the Church which transmits the Creed to us and, by its teaching, it is now, as it was from the beginning of the Church, the supreme norm which must be followed in the interpretation of Scripture and Tradition. Finally, by its Councils it decides all controversies.

The mere bandying about of isolated texts without regard to context and with little understanding of the rules for biblical interpretation can only lead to utter confusion and contradiction. Any interpretation of Sacred Scripture must be in accord with the analogy of Faith and with the fundamental law of all literary criticism, namely, that the author cannot be presumed to contradict himself. In the case of the Bible God Himself is the primary author.

	Albigensians
God	two gods, one good, one bad
God the Father	good god
God the Son	Christ, not god but an angel
Holy Spirit	a creature inferior to Christ, guardian of souls
Christ	an angel who had only the appearance of a man
Mary	not the mother of Christ
Creation	good god created spiritual good things bad god created material bad things
Evil	bad god created all material things which are bad
Sin	man has no free will
Original sin	Angels followed satan and are men's souls
Forgiveness of sin	*consolamentum* (only once)
Purgatory	No
Heaven	Purified souls alone
Mass	rejected
Sacraments	rejected them all

	Waldensians	Roman Catholics	
	one God	one God	
	First Person	First Person	Mystery* of the Holy Trinity
	Second Person	Second Person	
	Third Person	Third Person	
	Second person, who assumed a human nature, true God, true man	Second Person, who assumed a human nature, true God, true man	Mystery of the Incarnation
	Mother of Christ Mother of God	Mother of Christ Mother of God	
	God created all things good	God created all things good	
	man sinned at the suggestion of the devil	man sinned at the suggestion of the devil	
	man is responsible for his actions	man is responsible for his actions	
	Adam's sin stained all men's souls	Adam's sin stained all men's souls	
	Baptism Confess to anyone	Baptism Sacrament of Penance	
	No	Temporary abode after death where souls are purified	
	At death souls go to heaven or hell	Resurrected body and soul of the saved	
	once a year on Holy Thursday by those chosen for a period of time; not a matter of Orders	True sacrifice of the Body and Blood of Christ by an ordained priest	
	ambiguous; invalid if performed by an unworthy minister	Seven; ordinary minister has been ordained	

* A mystery is a truth that can only be known by God revealing

	Albigensians
Catholic Church	instrument of Satan; enemy of the truth; continuation of the synagogue
Church building	no
Prayer	The 'Our Father' only to be said by the Perfected
Prayers for the dead	No
Marriage	Evil
Ministers	Elected from among the Perfected; bishops
Oaths	All forbidden
Civil Authority	no right to punish
Preach	The Perfected
Crucifix	An abomination
Pilgrimages Statues	Worthless
Poverty	Perfected only; a very abstemious life
Religious Observances	Only the Perfected
John the Baptist	A devil
Death	Lacking *consolamentum* reincarnation
Resurrection of the body	No
Validity of the Bible	Only the New Testament

	Waldensians	Roman Catholics
	founded by Pope Sylvester I; it is a false and wicked church	Established by Christ to teach, govern, sanctify
	no	Consecrated place of public worship
	The 'Our Father' by everybody	The official liturgy of the Church and many public and private prayers by all
	Useless	Can assist the soul in purgatory
	Could be dissolved by mutual consent	A Sacrament; a holy vocation
	Elected for a specific period; not one of Orders	Pope, bishops, priests The Sacrament of Holy Orders
	All forbidden	Legitimate oaths
	No right to punish	Has right to enforce legitimate laws
	The Poor	Must receive permission from the local bishop
	Horrified because of Christ's sufferings; no reverence for it	A revered symbol of Christ's redemptive act
	Worthless	Aids to sanctification
	Absolute poverty for the Poor; equated poverty with holiness	A counsel, not mandatory; detachment from wordly goods is admirable
	Only the Poor	All without exception
		A saint
	Once, then judgment	Once, then judgment
	Yes	Yes
	Only the New Testament is of faith they quote Old Testament as times	Entire Bible

CHAPTER II
THE MEDIEVAL WORLD OF THE HIGH MIDDLE AGES

In a very real sense Europe of the twelfth and thirteenth centuries represented the culmination of the forces that created Western Civilization. Inheritors, however faintly at times, of the Graeco-Roman tradition of literature, philosophy and law, these settled, functioning peoples were making tremendous strides towards developing their own cultural brilliance. Enlivened by the Judaeo-Christian spirituality of a transcendent personal God the medieval man had a firm conviction of God's abiding interest in his personal dignity and destiny.

Religion, that viable relationship between God and man, was a prime preoccupation of the medieval man, the reason for his existence, the central fact that dominated his whole life.[1] There existed a basic agreement about God and how He should be worshiped. Europe was made up of a community of believers professing the same faith that, it was felt, was essential not only for the ecclesial community but for the body politic as well. To contemporaries the association and intermingling of the religious community and the civil and social world was highly desirable, indeed the normal way of life; this was the way things ought to be, had to be. And since unity of faith played such a central role in all facets of life, a heretic disassociated himself not only from the religious community but from the political and social community as well. He had declared himself a rebel!

This policy of basing political and social stability on the unity of faith characterized all societies of antiquity down through the Middle Ages - indeed too much so, for the pharaoh, king, emperor, etc. at times felt it necessary to declare himself a god in order to verify, legitimatize his authority to rule. This is the cutting edge of the distinction drawn by Christ: "Render to Caesar the things that are Caesar's, and to God the things that are God's." (Matthew

XXII,21) The two are not ultimately and radically the same. But the public conception of the necessity of the unity and consensus of religious as well as political principles was the ineluctable demand of all early empires, the Graeco-Roman world and the feudal ages. Thus Socrates was condemned to drink hemlock as a perverter of the morals of the youth. Why? Because he taught that there was only one god - and this in a polytheistic state! Similarly it was considered treason, *lèse-majesté,* to refuse adoration of the Roman gods and the imperial cult of Caesar. Hence for refusing, the Christians were thrown to the lions in the amphitheaters. The same reasoning explains Constantine's policy of preserving the state religion when Christianity succeeded paganism. This was the fundamental position of the empire: the necessity to maintain the inviolability of the state and religion. Multiple Constitutions in the Theodosian and Justinian Codes testify to the concern for orthodoxy. And this attitude continued throughout the Middle Ages.

With the decline of the Roman Empire under the hammering of the barbarian migrations, the *Pax Romana* supported by the magnificent Roman Law and organization gave way to decentralization and to a subsistence economy. The *cursus honorum* was succeeded by a more primitive lord-knight relationship wherein the knight's service protected the countryside and rallied once a year to serve the superior lord in defense of the larger domain. In theory all the functions of government operated through this system: king or suzerain - duke - count - viscount - baron, termed collectively, the nobility. The sinews that held society together were but tenuous and needed all the assistance that could be mustered to maintain a stable existence. The nobility by military service protected the area from outside molestation, while most of the civil arrangement was held together by customary law: the oath of homage by the noble to his liege lord on the one hand (feudalism), and the customary dues of the serf, the peasant, to his protecting knight for his support (manorialism). In such a rudimentary state, society required all the support possible. With so much greater reason, then, men of those times felt that the stability of all society depended on a general consensus on the feudal system and religious unity. So mutually supportive were both factors, it was agreed, that any deviation from the unity of faith spelled disintegration of the community.

The Catholic Church, for its part, fully sustained the efforts of the political authorities to advance the temporal welfare of all the people. In the spiritual realm the Church took very seriously its mission to teach, govern, and sanctify the faithful. In her language the Church is the union of all the faithful using common means - the Sacraments - to attain a common end - heaven - under a common authority - the Pope. Since, then, it had the duty of proclaiming the truths of Christ's doctrine, by the same token it had the corresponding responsibility of exposing heretical ideas and practices. The crime of heresy was defined as a deliberate denial of some article of revealed truth of the Catholic faith, and a public and obstinate persistence in that error. Through the centuries under the pressure of dissident elements the Church had more precisely delineated her official doctrine and condemned heretical teaching. Thus, at the first ecumenical Council at Nicaea in 325, she formally anathematized the Arian heresy which denied the divinity of Christ. The Council of Ephesus in 431 condemned the heresy of Nestorius which claimed that there were two separate persons in Christ, one divine and the other human, and, further, that Mary was the mother of the human person but not of the divine.

It was in accord with this tradition that the church attempted to deal with the dissident groups that had arisen in the period with which we are concerned, the late twelfth and the thirteenth centuries, particularly in southern France. The Albigensian and Waldensian sects had sprung up and made their presence felt throughout wide areas. From a comparison of their respective teachings, as described in Chapter One, with those of the Catholic Church, it is clear that the Church had a major problem on its hands.

There had been a number of heresies promoted by charismatic individuals in the previous century which flamed up and then flickered out, usually with the passing from the scene of the leader, e.g., Peter of Bruys, Henry the monk, Arnold of Brescia. But the Albigensians and the Waldensians were a different matter entirely, and their constant growth was a matter of grave concern for the local bishops and, with their manifest lack of success, to the civil authorities as well.

The condition of the Church in southern France.

The episcopate in Languedoc was in some ways a reflection of Provençal society. Some were saintly prelates attending to their duties assiduously. Others gave more attention to administration and the temporalities of their diocese with consequent neglect of the spiritual condition of their flock. Many of them had been chosen from the noble class and were not as concerned with the training and conduct of their parish priests as they should have been. Moreover the Gregorian Reform which among other things endeavored to withdraw the spiritual direction of the local church from the feudal grasp of lay appointees had had some effect. Expropriations of church property by feudal lords had been halted and some of the holdings returned to church administration. But with a few notable exceptions the church in Languedoc was anything but wealthy. For instance, the Bishop of Toulouse was in such straits that he had difficulty in obtaining the bare necessities of life.[2]

While some bishops made valiant efforts to care for their flock by countering the spread of false doctrines, others were much more lackadaisical. The response of some of the local bishops to the serious crisis caused by the rapid spread of Catharism and Waldensianism was something less than vigorous. Pope Alexander III in 1170 bluntly reprimanded the bishops for their culpable negligence. The parish priests were ill-prepared to meet the challenge. Aside from the usual horror stories repeated by modern authors - taking individual instances of clerical delinquencies and therefrom leaping to general condemnations - there are sufficient strictures in the letters of Pope Innocent III, the regional synods and the General Councils. The ordinary native clergy were far from the centers of learning and even from the minimal instruction of the *scholasticus* in the cathedral Chapter. Consequently the education of the local clergy was left to living in the rectory with the current pastor and learning from him the rudiments of Catholic doctrine and instruction in the administration of the Sacraments. One is reminded of the training of lawyers in the offices of practicing attorneys down to the twentieth century in the United States, "reading the law." On the other hand the monks and friars were much better trained in their monasteries and universities with their professors and libraries, and it would be to them, eventually, that the pope would have to go. But the universities were far from the countryside, and organized seminaries would have to wait till the reforms of the Council of Trent in the sixteenth century. For all that, it appears that the local clergy led their flocks along a fruitful spiritual path, as is evidenced from the piety of the times seen in the flourishing popular devotions, shrines, pilgrimages.[3]

Bernard of Clairvaux. In this increasingly grim situation it was only natural that the bishops would prevail upon the leading light of the twelfth century, Saint Bernard, to render assistance. He undertook a special preaching mission through the Midi, instructing the faithful and answering the attacks of the dissident sects. His success was short-lived, for upon his return to his monastery the Cathars continued to grow. A number of bishops who had brought Cathars to light and who were unable to convince them of their errors wrote to the abbot of Clairvaux for advice on what to do. His counsel was the standard policy of the church in all ages: not by arms but by arguments the errors should be refuted, and hopefully the wayward be reconciled to the faith. If, however, the heretic declines to repent, he is then to be admonished twice, and finally excommunicated, otherwise he will undermine the faith of others. He reprobated the hasty action of the secular power and the laity who in several instances had rushed off and summarily burned heretics without any reference to church authorities. On the other hand, St. Bernard, as St. Augustine before him, did approve resort to the secular power when all else failed in order to prevent irreparable damage to the orthodoxy of the laity. From personal experience and after years of counseling troubled prelates, the abbot of Clairvaux painted a very gloomy picture of the ravages of heresy in Languedoc:

> The churches are without priests; priests no longer receive proper respect; Christians deny Christ, and their temples pass for synagogues. They belittle the holiness of the sanctuary of God, and the Sacraments are no longer regarded as sacred. Feast Days pass without any solemnity; men die in their sins, and their souls are borne before the awe-inspiring tribunal without having been reconciled with God through the Sacrament of Penance, and without being fortified by Holy Viaticum. Children of Christians no longer know Christ and are not able anymore to walk in the way of salvation.[4]

Deeply troubled by the growing seriousness of the situation, a number of bishops gave strong emphasis to the persuasive approach. Preaching missions were increased. A major effort was launched under the aegis of the Papal Legate, Henry II of England and Louis VII of France. A large delegation of preachers accompanied by a military escort, because of the civil instability, toured Languedoc. But to little avail. They could not even free the bishop of Albi whom Roger II Trencavel held captive!

Political turmoil in the Midi

The Count of Toulouse was all too well positioned to appreciate and at times to profit from the tangled feudal interrelationships that mired that part of Europe. No less than four major suzerains laid claim to various parts of that area: the King of France, the King of England, the King of Aragon, and the Holy Roman Emperor. More bothersome at the moment, however, to Raymond V, Count of Toulouse, were the lesser Counts and Viscounts of the region: Roger Trencavel, Viscount of Béziers, Albi, and Carcassonne; Raymond-Roger, Count of Foix, and a number of lesser vassals in the Lauragais, Razès, Cabardes, Minervois, Biterrois, Agde, and Nimes. These latter had political ambitions of their own and at the same time sided with and aided the Cathars. Although not necessarily Cathars themselves they took the opportunity to brutalize priests, despoil church property, and burn churches and monasteries. Indeed the Count of Foix's sister, Esclarmonde, was a 'Perfected' as was Dame Cavaers, joint ruler of Fanjeaux with the Count of Foix. The lines of political authority in Languedoc were at best blurred, at worst mutually antagonistic, reducing a primitive judicial system to a state of paralysis. Further, this was the high Middle Ages and developing trade and commerce had introduced other elements into the legal system. The government of the city of Toulouse, for instance, was shared by the Count and a Consulate. Political power in Narbonne, Béziers, and Carassonne, was divided among bishops, viscounts, and consulates!

Feudalism almost from its origin spawned unruly, irregular military adventures. Where one class was entirely devoted to fighting, as were the knights of old, when they had no legitimate adversaries, then they proceeded to fight each other. Unemployed knights and other mercenaries descended into outright brigandage and plundering. The unprotected and the helpless were fair game and the local Church had long since tried its best to reduce this intolerable plague on society. Two devices in particular received popular acclaim. One, the Peace of God, required ever larger areas to swear to maintain peace and refrain from unlawful warfare. These pacts of peace were designed to protect people and property, ecclesiastical and lay, from these marauding bands. The other plan was the Truce of God whereby hostilities were to be halted during certain 'days of rest,' originally all Sundays, then it was extended from Wednesdays to sunrise on Mondays. Finally, it was lengthened to include Holy Seasons, e.g., Advent, the Octave of Christmas, until it lost its effect.

Routiers (brigands) and heretics.[5]

The civil disorder in the Midi was particularly corrosive and was incredibly worsened by the internecine strife of the Counts, Viscounts, and the towns themselves. But a specially odious threat was the presence of armed bands from outside the area who found this situation a fertile field for their depredations. Indeed they were often hired by nobles - and towns - to protect them and to do their fighting for them! In addition it appears that dissident religious groups took advantage of the opportunities at hand, and the association of the heretics and brigands became a commonplace. So much so that the Third Lateran (of 1179) as well as other councils linked the two together in a scathing denunciation of these foreign *routier* gangs and the heretics: Canon 27:

> With regard to the Barbatians, Aragonians, Basques, Navarese and others who practice such cruelty towards Christians that they respect neither churches nor monasteries, spare neither widows nor orphans, age nor sex, but after the manner of pagans destroy and lay waste everything, we decree likewise that those who hire or patronize them throughout the region in which they rave so madly, shall be publicly denounced in the

> churches on Sundays .... so long as they [the heretics] continue their iniquity.[6]

Perhaps the Count of Toulouse, Raymond V, described the general malaise best in his appeal to King Louis VII of France and to the General Chapter of the Cistercians asking for assistance against the alarming spread of Catharism.[7] This vile heresy, he stated, was breaking up families, and corrupting clerics to such an extent that churches were abandoned and falling into ruins, the Sacraments were scorned, the resurrection of the body denied, and the error of the two gods was being preached. He observed that while he had the power of the two swords, his major vassals had been infected with this heresy and had seduced a large part of the population, so that he himself was powerless. He raised a plea for help against this heresy whose poison was so virulent and the obduracy of its adherents so great that only God could conquer by force of arms. "Since the spiritual sword is absolutely useless, it is necessary to employ the material."

Action of the Church through regional and then ecumenical Councils.

In reality, strange as it may seem, the Church itself in the West had little experience in dealing with large, organized heretical sects, and as a result had no procedure ready at hand to cope with them. This may be accounted for by the fact that the individual heretics that had gathered somewhat of a following in the past were clerics and could be dealt with by ecclesiastical censure: deprivation of benefices, removal from office, expulsion from the monastery. Other aberrations were academic and usually did not spread beyond the halls of academe. Albigensianism and Waldensianism were quite otherwise, both because of the direct challenge of their doctrine, and the increasingly large numbers involved. Confronted with the daily perversion of the faithful, individual bishops were concerned with their responsibility to safeguard the faith in their diocese. Moreover they were perplexed as to the proper means to combat the diffusion of a heresy so damaging to the souls confided to their care.

Obviously more concerted action was called for and the changed atmosphere can be noticed between the Council of Tours in 1163 where the wide extent of the growth of heresy was noted and where the duty was laid upon the local clergy to search out heretics and hopefully recall them to their senses, and the Third Lateran Council in 1179 which condemned for the first time the heretics by name and encouraged the laity to join in the defense of the faith.

The first enactment of general legislation of the Church in regard to these heretics was the fourth canon of the Council of Tours:

> A damnable heresy has grown for a long time in Toulouse, spread to Gascony and other provinces and infected many people. This is why we order the bishops and priests of the country to direct their attention to this matter, to investigate these assemblies of heretics, and to see to it that the faithful offer no assistance to them or engage in any commerce with them.[8]

This decree did not name the heretics, much less describe their tenets. But it did take a significant step away from the private, accusatory method of denunciation - so characteristic of all previous canon and civil law - towards the appointment of a public official whose duty it would be to make an inquiry of the facts involved. This was almost by way of a suggestion, and nothing really eventuated, but it was a germ, and it would grow.

The next forceful action came from the Third Lateran Council of 1179. Canon 27 now named the heretics, described the seriousness of the situation, and requested vigorous counteraction:

> Though ecclesiastical discipline contents itself with spiritual judgment and does not inflict bloody punishments, it is, however, aided by the ordinances of Catholic princes, for men often seek a salutary remedy for their souls only when they fear some severe corporal punishment will be imposed upon them. Wherefore, since in Gascony, in the territory of Albi, in Toulouse and its neighborhood, and in some other places, the perversity of the heretics, whom some call Cathari, others Patarini, and others again Publicani, has assumed such proportions that they practice their wickedness no longer in secret as some do, but preach their error publicly and thus mislead the simple and the weak, we decree that they and all who defend and receive them are anathematized, and under penalty of anathema we forbid everyone to give them shelter, to admit them to his land, or to transact business with them.[9]

In the same Canon 27, the Council then went on to castigate the depredations of the marauding gangs, as we have already noted, and requested the princes and all the people to take up arms against 'such pests.' Still no practical methods were proposed to put these provisions into effect - other than all out war!

Joint condemnation of the heretics by the Pope and the Emperor.

In 1184 at Verona in Italy, Pope Lucius III and the Emperor, Frederick Barbarossa, jointly issued an important decree, *Ad abolendam,*[10] condemning heresy and heretics. By name were denounced the Cathars and the Waldensians. Four general catagories of heretics were enumerated:

— those who preached without permission from the local bishop (e.g., the Waldensians)

— those whose teachings differed from that of the Roman Church (the classic definition of heresy)

— those excommunicated by the local bishop for heresy

— those who defended or assisted the heretics

Local bishops were instructed to make an official visitation, once or twice a year, of every parish in their diocese where heretics were reputed to live, either personally or through a representative assisted by honest and capable men. In each parish the bishop was required to request three or more trustworthy men to report under oath any heretical activities that had come to their attention. If anyone declined to take the oath, that very fact would make him suspect since the Cathars and the Waldensians as an article of belief repudiated all oaths for whatever purpose. The inquiry completed, the accused were to be cited before the bishop's tribunal.

From this point on the process is somewhat vague. It was possible that the accused could clear himself by the accepted methods of the customary law. Otherwise the bishop would convene his court. As a judge he took into consideration the gravity of the offense and the circumstances relevant to the person involved. If the heretic was a cleric he might be permitted to purge himself by spontaneously and immediately returning to the unity of the faith by publicly abjuring his errors and by giving guarantees of his sincerity. Otherwise he was to be degraded, deprived of all offices and benefices, and be handed over to the secular arm for due punishment, *animadversione debita puniendus.* Laymen were able to purge themselves by abjuring heresy, by giving pledges of their sincerity, and by promptly returning to the orthodox faith. Relapsed heretics were to be handed over summarily to the secular arm for due punishment as their first conversion was now regarded as insincere. Due punishment, at this time, meant exile and the confiscation of one's property. All incurred the canonical and civil stigma of infamy (*infamia*), a legal term debarring a person from obtaining any ecclesiastical office or dignity, from pleading in court or giving testimony, and from exercising any public office. In their turn the counts, barons, podestas, and consuls of all cities were required to take a special oath to assist faithfully and effectively church authorities against the heretics when called upon. Furthermore by reason of their office they were ordered to execute assiduously the mandates of ecclesiastical and imperial Constitutions.

However detailed this decree may seem to be, it did not represent anything radically new. The local bishop always had had the duty of canonically visiting the parishes of his diocese - as he does today - and of protecting his flock from the ravages of false doctrine. Even the denunciations against heretical suspects do not originate with the bishop himself. Rather they are the result of public scandal, reports, rumors adduced by sworn witnesses. Hence the procedure remained basically accusatory by private citizens. However this imperial Constitution did extend the process throughout the empire. The success of the procedure herein outlined depended in large measure upon a close cooperation of both clerical and lay officials. Hence the significance of the adherence of the emperor to this papal decree, for without secular assistance nothing much was going to happen.

Results. The real question here, as in so much of medieval legislation, is: what happened? what practical effect did *Ad abolendam* have? In practice, it seems, it had little or no effect. For all the formidable nature of the decree it apparently remained a dead letter. What is true, however, is that heresy grew apace and became more menacing than ever.

The role of Pope Innocent III (1198-1216)

As Innocent assumed the duties of the papacy he was faced with a critical situation in Languedoc and Provence. As he saw it from Rome, the negligence of some bishops and the indifference of the nobles had combined to permit a devastating spread of Catharism. A canon lawyer and an administrator of the first rank, Innocent addressed himself to the task of protecting the faithful from false doctrine, while at the same time attempting by compassion and persuasion to reconcile the heretics to the church. Although the unsettling growth of heresy was a serious concern of this busy pontiff it was by no means his only preoccupation. The Crusade to the Holy Land; the defense of the Church against the encroachments of feudal lords; the reform of the Roman Curia, the monasteries, the episcopate and the clergy; the reconciliation of the Greek Church; the perennial tilting with the emperor, all of these projects constantly claimed his attention.

Nevertheless, the pope applied himself to this challenging undertaking with a will. His over-riding concern was to stop the diffusion of heresies which were misleading the souls confided by God to the Church's care and to bring the erring back to the practice of the true faith. Anything less had to be considered a failure. This he hoped to accomplish by dispatching well-trained preachers into this area, by encouraging the bishops to bend every effort towards eradicating this cancerous growth, by correcting clerical deficiencies, and by enforcing legislation already on the books. For Innocent III believed implicitly in the power of the Word, provided it was propounded in a competent and effective way. His policy was to be one of "persuasion" rather than of "coercion."

Towards this end he sent two Cistercian monks, Guy and Rainier, into Languedoc and Provence within months of his election in April, 1198. He informed the local bishops, counts, barons and all the faithful that he was sending these two monks to preach there because the Cathars, Waldensians, and other heretics had multiplied so much that they had seduced many of the faithful and corrupted them with the poison of their doctrine. He enjoined all the above to assist the Cistercians in their efforts. In spite of two more letters to the same affect, the mission of the papal legates lagged.

A year later, in March 1199, Innocent III issued a severe decretal, *Vergentis in senium,*[11] in which he compared heresy to the crime of treason in Roman Law. In this decree he authorized the confiscation of the property of convicted heretics. For, he reasoned, if in Roman Law those guilty of *lèse-majesté,* a capital offense, were deprived of their possessions, how much worse was it to offend the Divine Majesty by straying from the true faith of Jesus Christ than to affront a temporal ruler. To enforce this policy the pope dispatched John, cardinal of Saint Prisca; later in the same year he enlarged the cardinal's mission to include an investigation into the sad state of affairs in the archbishopric of Narbonne, where, Innocent had heard:

> the priests were being treated shamelessly and the insolence of the tyrants was flaunting itself in mockery even in the sanctuary of the Lord. Laymen were transforming churches into fortresses where Christians engage in forays and war against Christians. The bishops know this but were ignoring it.[12]

In scathing language he reproved the bishops for their failure to select and train proper candidates for the priesthood and for not maintaining due vigilance over their dioceses.

Despite these handicaps, the pope continued his exertions to restore the region to the true faith by sending yet another mission to preach the orthodox doctrine in 1204. Again he called upon the Cistercians. The abbot of Citeaux himself, Arnold-Aimery, and two other monks from the Cistercian monastery of Fontfroide, Peter of Castelnau and Ralph, responded to the papal appeal for help. At Carcassonne they engaged in a public debate with a Cathar bishop, Bertrand of Simorre. The King of Aragon, Peter, who presided, adjudged the Cathars to be in error - but to little practical avail. The Cistercians became very discouraged and wanted to withdraw. Innocent III reassured them, but at this stage he himself was none too optimistic.

At this juncture, undaunted Saint Dominic proposed a different approach. He suggested to the pope that the Catholic preachers adopt the method that Christ had laid out for his disciples:

> Provide no gold, no second coat, no shoes, no stick, no silver or copper to fill your purse, no pack for the road; the worker earns his keep. (Matthew X,9-10)

— the very method utilized so effectively by the Cathar Perfected. The legates[13] in Languedoc accepted this procedure and broke up into separate groups. At Pamiers some of the Waldensians, led by Durand of Huesca, returned to the Roman Church. The pope received them kindly in Rome. He approved their group as a religious congregation and gave them permission to preach since a number of them were clerics already well instructed and prepared for this task. He reminded them, however, of the power of the local bishop to authorize preachers in his diocese - as was then, and still is, the ordinary law of the church. Innocent III had to defend the new religious community (the former Poor Men of Lyons) from the suspicions of both the bishops and the papal legates in southern France. He instructed them that if the new religious community needed correction from time to time the bishops should do so with compassion and kindness. A number of the Poor Lombards under the leadership of Bernard Prim were also restored to full communion with Rome a few years later.

All in all, however, in spite of the prodigious efforts expended, progress remained agonizingly slow.

Innocent III removes bishops.[14]

Meanwhile, finding that his exhortations to the bishops at times gained little response the pope proceeded to renovate the hierarchy of southern France.

— The Bishop of Fréjus was removed for incompetence.

— The Bishop of Carsassonne was retired because of advanced age and his inability to carry out his duties.

— The Bishop of Béziers, William de Roquessels, was summarily deposed for disobedience in not excommunicating the heretical Consuls after he had promised to do so.

— The pope ordered the Archbishop of Embrun and the Abbot of Boscodon to investigate the evil reports concerning Peter, Bishop of Vence, and to depose him if the charges were found to be verified.

— Innocent III ordered the election of a new bishop for Viviers because his legates, Raoul and Peter of Castelnau in the course of their preaching mission had found his bishopric in lamentable condition. By reason of being a noble and powerful, Nicholas, Bishop of Viviers, was able to retain the title but a new bishop was ordered to be selected.

— The Bishop of Agde was accused of serious delinquencies but on appeal to Rome was permitted to remain in office until his death in 1213.

— The Bishop of Toulouse, Raymond de Rabastens, was ousted for simony by the papal legates, though the pope allowed him to continue some purely ceremonial functions.

— The Archbishop of Auch was deposed.

— The Bishop of Valence was dismissed.

— The Bishop of Rodez was removed.

— Berenger, Archbishop of Narbonne, who amply qualified for similar action, used all the means at his disposal to remain in office. He personally went to Rome to appeal his cause. The pope as always treated him kindly and believed his promises, but eventually had to remove him.

As replacements for the deposed bishops Innocent III, for the most part, drew upon the Cistercians and other monks and well qualified priests. In addition he directed local synods to be held at Avignon, Saint-Gilles, Narbonne, Arles, Pamiers, Lavaur and Montpellier at which the duties and life-styles of Bishops, priests, and monks were spelled out in some detail. All this was by way of a spiritual renovation from within! By these decisive actions the Holy See hoped to remedy some of the conditions that permitted the rise of heresy. Unfortunately for Innocent III and his successors in the papacy, this purge did not achieve its purpose fully for the simple reason that the deportment of the clergy was not so much the cause of heresy as it was an indication of the spirit of the age.

Assassination of the Papal Legate.

Unhappily, the flow of events was radically changed by the sudden murder of the papal legate, Peter of Castelnau, by an unknown knight on January 14, 1208. The day before, an acrimonious exchange had passed between Raymond VI, Count of Toulouse, and the legate during which altercation the Count had repeatedly threatened the legate that wherever he went he would be under the Count's constant surveillance. Shades of Thomas à Becket!

The Fourth Lateran Council, 1215.

For some time it had been the intention of Innocent III to assemble a General Council to deal with two matters that lay close to his heart: the regaining of the Holy Land and the internal reform of the Church. In a letter to all of the dioceses of the Church he wrote:

> I have decided after the manner of the ancient fathers to convoke a General Council by means of which evils may be uprooted, virtues implanted, mistakes extirpated, the faith strengthened, disputes adjusted, peace established, liberty protected, Christian princes and people induced to aid the Holy Land, and salutary decrees enacted for the higher and lower clergy.[15]

This call went forth two and a half years before the actual convocation of the Council. In the meanwhile preliminary investigations and reports on the needs of each diocese were prepared and sent to Rome. When the greatest Council of the Middle Ages assembled the agenda was already well prepared and the three sessions of the Council were completed within the month of November. Present were the patriarchs of Constantinople and Jerusalem, some 412 bishops, 800 abbots and priors, delegates of the patriarchs of Alexandria, Antioch, the emperor Frederick II, and Henry the Latin Emperor of Constantinople, as well as delegates of the Kings of England, France, Aragon, Hungary and Jerusalem. Seventy decrees were approved and promulgated by the pope covering matters of dogma, morals, discipline and organization.

Actually there was little new in the decisions. For the most part, the decrees merely codified and confirmed the instructions of the previous popes and provincial synods. In regard to the prevailing heresies, Canon 1 (as we have seen in Chapter One), spelled out in detail the traditional teaching of the Church with particular reference to the aberrations of the Albigensians and the Waldensians.

Canon 3: We excommunicate and anathematize every heresy that raises itself against the holy, orthodox and Catholic faith which we have above explained; condemning all heretics under whatever names they may be known .... Those condemned, being handed over to the secular rulers or their bailiffs, let them be abandoned, to be punished with due justice, clerics being first degraded from their orders. As to the property of the condemned, if they are laymen, let it be confiscated; if clerics, let it be applied to the churches from which they received revenues. But those who are only suspected, due consideration being given to the nature of the suspicion and the character of the person, unless they prove their innocence by a proper defense, let them be anathematized and avoided by all until they have made suitable satisfaction; but if they have been under excommunication for one year, then let them be condemned as heretics. Secular authorities, whatever office they may hold, shall be admonished and induced and if necessary compelled by ecclesiastical censure, that as they wish to be esteemed and numbered among the faithful, so for the defense of the faith they ought publicly to take an oath that they will strive in good faith and to the best of their ability to exterminate in the territories subject to their jurisdiction all heretics pointed out by the Church .... But if a temporal ruler, after having been requested and admonished by the Church, should neglect to cleanse his territory of this heretical foulness, let him be excommunicated .... If he refuses to make satisfaction within a year, let the matter be made known to the supreme pontiff, that he may declare the ruler's vassals absolved from their allegiance and may offer the territory to be ruled by Catholics ....; the right, however, of the chief ruler is to be respected so long as he offers no obstacle in this matter and permits freedom of action ....

We decree that those who give credence to the teachings of the heretics, as well as those who receive, defend, and patronize them, are excommunicated; and we firmly declare that after any one of them has been branded with excommunication, if he has deliberately failed to make satisfaction within a year, let him incur *ipso facto* the stigma of infamy and let him not be admitted to public offices or deliberations, and let him not take part in the election of others to such offices or use his right to give testimony in a court of law. Let him also be intestable, that he may not have the free exercise of making a will, and let him be deprived of the right of inheritance. Let no one be urged to give an account to him in any matter, but let him be urged to give an account to others. If perchance he be a judge, let his decisions have no force, nor let any cause be brought to his attention. If he be an advocate, let his assistance by no means be sought. If a notary, let the instruments drawn up by him be considered worthless, for, the author being condemned, let them enjoy a similar fate ....

If any refuse to avoid such after they have been ostracized by the Church, let them be excommunicated till they have made suitable satisfaction. Clerics shall not give the sacraments of the Church to such pestilential people, nor shall they presume to give them Christian burial, or to receive their alms or offerings ....

But since some, under "the appearance of godliness, but denying the powers thereof," as the Apostle says (II Timothy III,5), arrogate to themselves the authority to preach, as the same Apostle says: "How shall they preach unless they be sent?" (Romans X,15), all those prohibited or not sent, who, without authority of the Apostolic See or of the Catholic bishop of the locality, shall presume to usurp the office of preaching either publicly or privately, shall be excommunicated .... We add, moreover, that every archbishop or bishop should himself or through his archdeacon or some other suitable persons, twice or at least once a year make the rounds of his diocese in which report has it that heretics dwell, and there compel three or more men of good charcter or, if it should be deemed advisable, the entire neighborhood, to swear that if anyone knows of the presence there of heretics or others holding secret assemblies, or differing from the common way of the faithful in faith or morals, they will make them known to the bishop. The latter shall then call together before him those accused, who, if they do not purge themselves of the matter of which they are accused, or if after the rejection of their error they lapse into their former wickedness, shall be canonically punished. But if any of them by damnable obstinacy should disapprove of the oath and should perchance be unwilling to swear, from this very fact let them be regarded as heretics.[16]

Canon 6 ordered provincial synods to be held annually for the correction of abuses. Following canons reminded bishops of their obligation to make certain that they or their representatives instruct the faithful in the doctrine of the church. Clerics were warned against incontinence, drunkenness, and unbecoming behavior. Further to make sure of the proper selection and training of priests the previous decrees mandating a competent teacher be provided for this purpose were confirmed.

Canon 18 stated flatly: "No one shall bestow any blessing in judicial tests or ordeals by hot or cold water or hot iron," - thus effectively vacating that method of determining guilt or innocence.

Types of ecclesiastical trials for delinquent clerics.

Finally in order to guarantee the effectiveness of the decrees of this Council, Canon 8 empowered religious superiors to investigate reports of serious irregularities of prelates and clerics. The Canon noted three types of procedure:

I. Accusation (*accusatio*). An individual enters charges in writing against a prelate or cleric and at the same time binds himself in writing to undergo the same penalty that would have been imposed on the accused if in the course of the investigation or trial his charges should be proved groundless (*Lex talionis*). This was to prevent malicious or spiteful accusations made to embarrass prelates or clerics.

II. Denunciation (*denunciatio*). An individual reveals a crime to the religious superior of the accused, but only after repeated admonitions have been ignored. The accuser is not amenable to the law of reprisal.

III. Inquiry, inquest (*inquisitio*). In this type the religious superior himself undertakes to make an investigation after complaints and evil reports have reached his ears.

The importance of this Canon 8 is not so much its confirmation of long standing Canon Law for the trials of *clerics* (not heretics), but because it will be the procedure adopted by Pope Gregory IX some fifteen years later for the inauguration of the Inquisition and because of its appropriation by civil criminal law down to the French Revolution!

Innocent III dies.

Within a year after the adjournment of the "Great Council," as it was known, Pope Innocent III was dead. Among his many projects, he had energetically devoted himself to the solution of the problem of the spread of heresy in Languedoc and elsewhere. He firmly believed that the preaching of sound doctrine would protect the faithful on the one hand, and bring back the wandering dissidents on the other. He recognized the negligence of some of the bishops and acted forthrightly to correct it. He admonished and encouraged the diocesan clergy to live up to their priestly office, and he took measures to assist in their proper selection and training. He treated the erring compassionately, but firmly, specifying that the teachings of each heretical group should be properly indicated and that the orthodox not be labeled as heretics, e.g., some of the Humiliati. New laws he did not make. He simply codified and tried to enforce those already enacted. He added no new punishments. But his good start, particularly with the aid of the well-trained monks and friars, was interrupted and thwarted by the continuing civil disorders, and, more proximately, by the murder of the papal legate, Peter of Castelnau. Thus historical forces reversed the trend, and the Albigensian Crusade brought the use of stronger measures until in a more orderly, tranquil environment peaceful spiritual procedures could be resumed once again.

The Albigensian Crusade (1209-1229).[17]

An enormous amount of ink has been passionately spilled by

otherwise well-balanced historians on the alleged atrocities and extensive slaughtering of the innocent in this Crusade through southern France. "Kill all! Kill all! for God will know his own," was the supposed instructions of the papal legate to the inquiring crusaders at Béziers where 7,000 old men, women and children are reported to have been slain in a single church, La Madeleine, and 20,000 inhabitants are said to have been massacred in a town which held at the most liberal estimate eight or nine thousand. These oft-repeated horror stories have built a legend that has passed for history down to our own enlightened century. That the facts do not substantiate the charges does not disturb those who trumpet these tales.

The ultimate responsibility for having called the crusade rests with the reigning Roman Pontiff. Whatever may have been the motives of the feudal nobles in joining, opposing, or merely using the crusade it is to Rome that one must look for the reasons why the knights of northern France were summoned to ride south. As we have seen, the papacy had labored for almost a half century to instruct the faithful more adequately in the truths of their faith, to protect them from the contagion of false doctrine, and to reconcile dissidents to the Roman Church. It had utilized all its traditional methods: preaching missions, papal legates making their rounds, local and provincial synods, special efforts by St. Bernard and other Cistercians and by St. Dominic. All this had been tried over and over again with but a modicum of success. Repeated appeals for the cooperation of the secular rulers had for one reason or another all come to naught. It was only when Innocent III became convinced of the paralysis of the public powers and of the local churches that he resorted to a crusade. The imminence of complete domination by the Albigensians, the inertia of the king, the impotence and bad will of the princes, the complicity of a great number of local nobles who had permitted the Cathars to flourish, the exposed position of the laity, the repulse of the papal missions, the lost prestige of the religious leaders, the ineffectiveness of spiritual methods swamped by the unrestrained devastation of brigands and mercenaries - and now the murder of the papal legate, Peter of Castelnau - all combined to force the conclusion on the mind of the pope that military constraint alone could restore public order and thus permit the peaceful pursuit of the people's spiritual welfare.

Having made this bitter decision, Innocent had a major task in rousing the political sovereigns to action. The kings of France and England eyed each other malevolently; Spain always thought in terms of the Moors; the Emperor, Frederick II (not yet crowned) was equivocal, depending on the current status of his relations with the pontiff and the city states. As it happened, none of them volunteered, although Philip Augustus of France, with a notable lack of enthusiasm, did permit a limited number of his nobles - no more than 500 he said - to go south. At the same time he entered a demurrer in reference to the transfer of feudal lands from heretics to faithful lords, for he possessed suzerain rights. Nevertheless a fair number of nobles responded to the preaching of the crusade: Odo, Duke of Burgundy; the Counts of Nevers, St. Pol and Boulogne; a number of prelates, including the archbishops of Rheims, Rouen and Sens; and members of the lesser nobility. The king of France begged off heading the crusade himself, so that the papal legates themselves had to assume control of the host until the nobles could choose one of the lords to be the commander. Meantime Raymond VI of Toulouse, seeing the lay of the land, hastened to ask the pope for reconciliation. Innocent III, as always, listened to his plea, dispatched his secretary Milo to ascertain if Raymond was sincere, and astonishingly, accepted his promise to remedy the faults charged against him. The list of accusations against the Count was indeed formidable: that he had not expelled heretics from his territories but had favored them; that he had appropriated church lands, fortified churches, vandalized monasteries and churches, and abused the clergy and even bishops, e.g., of Carpentras and of Vaison; that he had employed brigands and *routiers*; that he was at least guilty of complicity in the murder of Peter of Castelnau. All these things and others Raymond VI promised to rectify - as he had sworn to do numerous times before, and then ignored. Absolved from the ban of the church he promptly joined the crusaders. Some have suggested that he did this to keep the crusaders away from his own lands and directed towards those of his unruly vassals, the Trencavels!

And that in fact is exactly what happened. The initial drive of the crusaders was into the territories of Raymond Roger, Viscount of Béziers and Carcassonne and lord of the Albigeois and of Razès. His holdings covered a large area of Languedoc including the towns of Béziers, Carcassonne and Albi - encompassing the heaviest concentration of heretics in the Midi. For these lands the Trencavels did homage to Raymond VI of Toulouse and to King Peter II of Aragon: a good example of the tangled feudal arrangements in the region. At the moment, Raymond Roger was at odds with Raymond of Toulouse and decided to make a stand against the crusaders by building up the defenses of Carcassonne while encouraging Béziers to look out for itself. As the crusaders approached Béziers its defenders made the tactical blunder of making a sortie which left one of its gates undefended. The foot soldiers of the advancing host overran the town and killed with abandon, apparently without regard for age or sex, on July 22, 1209. Carcassonne was next, and after a two week siege Raymond Roger surrendered permitting the people to depart unharmed while he gave himself up as hostage.

With the envelopment of most of the lands of the Trencavels the first advance of the crusaders was nearly completed. It was high time for the papal legates to bow out and for a noble to assume the leadership of the crusade. Most of the northern lords declined the offer (many thanks, but no thanks), and somewhat reluctantly Simon de Montfort of the Île-de-France was prevailed upon to direct operations. He had already participated in the Fourth Crusade, distinguishing himself by refusing to join in the attack on Zara, a Christian city. On his return from the Holy Land he had answered the call to deal with disorder and heresy in Languedoc. Now under pressure from the Duke of Burgundy and other nobles he consented to lead the crusade on the condition that the aforesaid nobles would come to his assistance if he needed them. De Montfort knew from experience that after the feudal host had completed its customary forty days of annual feudal service, the knights would return north leaving him in a precarious situation.

With only some thirty knights to assist him Simon de Montfort experienced a difficult winter, 1209-1210, as stronghold after stronghold broke their agreements with him. With the spring his wife was able to send him reinforcements from the north, and he gradually regained both the lost towns and additional ones. This situation changed but little until Simon's death. The supposed "land grab" by the northern lords of the lush pastures of the Midi remains to be sustained. They were only too happy to ride back north after their forty days of service, as the chronicler tells us, because they had no desire to remain and be killed in the south.[18] Indeed Simon had to double his knights' wages in order to induce them to remain with him. Despite these difficulties Montfort seemed to be making progress towards more friendly and enduring relations with the southerners, only to be thwarted by repeated violations of peace treaties. Thus Aimery of Montreal twice made peace with Simon and twice broke his word. As a result when Aimery led the defense of Lavaur, Montfort did not spare him or his followers a third time. They were unceremoniously dispatched along with a number of heretics who were burned.

Throughout all these skirmishes only a handful of knights participated, at most a few hundred, though the chroniclers always speak in figures of thousands. Finally King Peter II of

Aragon decided to join forces with the Counts of Toulouse, Foix and Comminges. In a little town south of Toulouse, Muret, one of the few major battles of the crusade took place, September 12, 1213. Montfort, being out-numbered by perhaps 2,000 to 4,000 to his 1,000, concluded that his only chance lay in going onto the attack in the open field. His tactics succeeded beyond belief. The opposing forces became disorganized, some deserted - Raymond VI did not show up - and Peter II was slain. This, the most decisive engagement of the crusade, effectively removed Aragon from further involvement in the struggle.

The territorial dispositions were made at the Fourth Lateran Council in Rome, 1215. Simon de Montfort was invested with all the lands of the Count of Toulouse, while Raymond's son retained the marquisate of Provence. These provisions did not sit well with Raymond VI. He had been deprived of his ancestral lands on the grounds of harboring heretics - and he and his son spent the next ten years, 1215-1225, gradually winning them back. Town after town began to rally to the side of Raymond, who was joined by Roger Bernard of Foix, Bernard IV of Comminges and by lesser nobles of the Toulousain. Together they seized Toulouse and held out against the assault of Montfort who was killed before the walls, June 25, 1218.

Simon of Montfort was succeeded by his son, Amalric, who was unable to prevent the gradual disintegration of his holdings. He tried to hand over his lands to King Philip Augustus, but to no avail. Finally, the new king, Louis VIII, undertook a crusade in the south in 1226 and reversed the flow of events once more. The final peace treaty was signed at Paris, April 12, 1229. Herein, indeed, the political arrangements in the popular mind overshadow the religious commitments, for, aside from a few temporary provisions, Languedoc was permanently joined to the kingdom of France in fact as well as in name. But the purpose of the pope's summoning of the crusade in the first place was achieved: the installation of responsible rulers in Languedoc who could and would insure peace and order and would suppress heresy. Of the thirty-one clauses of the treaty, the first six directly concerned the suppression of heresy, the rights of the church, restitution of property, and security guarantees. It must be said, however, that while the political clauses were effective, the provisions against heresy were not.

As far as the traditional procedure of the church towards instructing the faithful and guarding them against the corrosion of heretical doctrines, the Albigensian Crusade represented an interruption, but so long as political and religious chaos persisted in Languedoc any other method of approach was hopeless. Now that political stability had been more or less achieved, religious reconstruction had a fair chance of success. The Cathars and the Waldensians were alive and flourishing, but the support and protection of the nobility had been neutralized. Further, the political lines were no longer purely feudal. The rising power of organized citizenry, as demonstrated in town after town during the crusade, gave notice that they were a power to be reckoned with.

Pope Honorius III (1216-1227).

As sometimes happens, an administrator of lesser stature and activity may achieve more in certain areas than a more brilliant man. And so it was with Honorius III who saw an end to the Albigensian Crusade and received the active legal cooperation of the Kings of France and Aragon and the Emperor - which Innocent III did not have. The decrees of the Fourth Lateran Council now appeared in the legal codes of all three, along with their individual prescriptions of a less acceptable nature. In 1224 Frederick II decreed the stake for heretics in Lombardy, but apparently the only time this edict received any attention it failed, and the official attempting to apply it very nearly lost his own life. It remained in effect a dead letter.[19]

It is also fair to say, however, that the efforts of the past half century to deal with the problem of heresy had not achieved success. The successor to Honorius III in the papacy came to the conclusion that papal authority would have to lend support to competently trained experts circulating in the infected regions, using a uniform procedure under a centrally organized administration. The new pope, Gregory IX (1227-1241), set about to establish the Inquisition.

CHAPTER III
THE ESTABLISHMENT OF THE INQUISITION (1231/33)

The papal Inquisition, properly so-called, originated with Pope Gregory IX (1227-1241). The Inquisition was an extraordinary court of exception established by the papacy to investigate and adjudicate persons accused of heresy. It was a rational inquiry by special officials appointed by and responsible to the Holy See. The purpose was to bring order and legality to the procedure for dealing with heresy, since, on the one hand, the attitude in southern France was one of benign indifference or even approval of heresy, while in the north, on the other hand, particularly in Germany, there was the tendency to burn alleged heretics forthwith. While the inquisitors worked in cooperation with the local bishops, their authority derived directly from Rome, which now chose to exercise primary jurisdiction over heresy and heretics. Although many profess to see the origin of the Inquisition in previous Councils and synods, these regulations pertained to the ordinary duties of the local bishops, who always had this responsibility along with all the other demands of their office. Now for the first time, Gregory IX created a new procedure whereby an office was established whose primary and only function was the searching out of heresy and the resolution of the findings. It was both a new procedure, a rational inquiry by a judge, and new a institution, a papal agency designed to ultilize this new procedure for uncovering and trying alleged heretics.

The pope was quite well aware of all the efforts that had gone before — and that they had not succeeded. Now, with conditions considerably modified, he was able to enact legislation himself with the assurance of having the active support of the secular powers and the aid of the newly founded mendicant Orders, the Dominicans and the Franciscans. The consequent close association and correspondence between the pope and the inquisitors in the field made for the gradual crystallization of a definite procedure and clearly defined juridical processes. The stress and strain of meeting and dealing with individual problems that arose out of the trials of heretics necessitated the sending of inquiries to Rome for solution. It was from the replies of the popes and of regional meetings of bishops to these questions of the inquisitors that the legal code and form of the Inquisition developed.

The actual evolution of the Inquisition as an institution may be observed in three steps. First, Pope Gregory IX in February, 1231, issued a general constitution excommunicating all heretics in general, and the Cathars, Patarenes, the Poor Men of Lyons, Passagians, Josephines, Arnaldists and Speronists in particular.[1] This decree specified that suspects were to be examined by church officials (inquisitors) and if they remained adamant in their heresy they were to be handed over to a secular judge who would impose the civil penalties. Persons who assisted or defended heretics were to be excommunicated and declared 'infamous'. Those only suspected of heresy could clear themselves by accepted methods, i.e., compurgation.

The second landmark document, going far towards implementing the Inquisition, followed closely upon Gregory IX's decree above and was obviously inspired by it. The head of the civil government of Rome, Senator Annibale, in the same month, February, 1231, enacted similar legislation, in practically the same words, specifying that the examination and decision in regard to heresy must be made by "inquisitors appointed by the church."[2] The penalties laid down in civil law for the convicted heretic were exile and confiscation of property, one third to the person preferring the charge, one third to the Senator, and one third for the repair of the city walls. Legal 'infamy' was imposed on those who actively cooperated with heretics.

The following year, 1232, the Emperor, Frederick II, in

identical language laid down an imperial constitution ordering the civil officials to render all assistance to "the inquisitors appointed by the Apostolic See."[3] Louis IX, king of France, had already made his position abundantly clear in the Treaty of Paris, April 12, 1229, which concluded the Albigensian Crusade. A large number of provisions of this treaty detailed the actions to be taken by Count Raymond VII against heretics in southern France, pointing to their complete expulsion from the territory. The king himself in the ordonnance *Cupientes* of Easter 1229 not only reinforced his father's laws providing for civil disabilities for convicted heretics and the confiscation of their property, but also ordered all feudal officials of the realm to take an active part in searching out heretics. "We order all the lords and officers to make every effort with diligence and fidelity to search out and uncover heretics ...."[4] When they were found, heretics were to be remanded to the ecclesiastical authorities. James I of Aragon in Spain enacted similar legislation, so that the active cooperation of the secular authority in the immediate areas was assured.

The third milestone in the definitive establishment of the Inquisition was the appointment of the mendicant Friars to be the actual officals who were to carry out papal instructions. With the selection of such highly trained preachers, specially skilled in the knowledge of Sacred Scripture and theology, Gregory IX was able to organize a more thoroughgoing, continuous campaign of explaining the true doctrine of the church to all the faithful, answering charges alleged against it, and seeking out and weighing the evidence laid against persons accused of heresy. The newly founded Dominicans and Franciscans came to hand just at this time. With a strong academic training in theology, the Friars were the first to bridge the gap between the university world and pastoral care. Dedicated to poverty, chastity, and obedience, they were particularly well suited to counterbalance the austerities of the Cathar 'Perfected,' and the simplicity of the Poor Men of

Lyons. Further, they could devote their full attention to this most important apostolate. Since they received their jurisdiction directly from the pope, they could eschew the complicated interrelationships of the feudal nobility and the hierarchy. They were, in a word, not only preachers and investigators but judges as well — Inquisitors in the fullest sense of the term. The Order of Friars Preachers, founded by St. Dominic, and the Order of Friars Minor, established by St. Francis of Assisi, were requested by the pope to undertake this arduous task — which others before them had undertaken with precious little success.

In 1232 the Dominican Alberic was already exercising jurisdiction in Lombardy under the title of "inquisitor of heretical depravity." However the first general mandate of Gregory IX requesting the Dominicans to commence a general inquisition in the provinces of southern France was issued on April 20, 1233. Two days later the pope instructed the Dominican Provincial (Religious Superior) in Toulouse to appoint friars learned in theology to travel throughout the area on a preaching mission, hopefully to bring erring souls back to the fold, but to proceed in any event to enforce papal statutes in regard to the recalcitrant.[5] Among the first Dominicans so named were Peter Seila, William Arnold, and Pons of St. Gilles. The first Franciscan inquisitor recorded by name was Friar Stephen of Saint Thibéry, 1235-1242. Professor Fredericq regards the bull of Pope Innocent IV on January 13, 1246 as the first general mandate to the Friars Minor, but we have ample evidence of the work of the Franciscans in Germany long before that date. Shortly afterwards, the pope sent the Dominicans and the Franciscans into Germany, Spain and Lombardy as well, but the bulk of their work was performed in the provinces of southern France. Robert called the Bougre, a Dominican nominated by Gregory IX, April 29, 1233, as inquisitor-general for France, operated as a special appointee. Lacking sufficient supervision, he was led into excesses, reportedly burning 180 persons in 1239. Reports of his outrageous conduct finally reached the pope, and he was forthwith deposed and imprisoned for life in a monastery. Much the same must be said of Conrad of Marburg, a priest deputed to combat heresy in Germany. He too conducted himself in a high-handed manner, to say the least, and was assassinated for his efforts in 1233.

In general, however, the Inquisitors themselves, the Dominicans and Franciscans, while eminently well qualified for the task, found it difficult and burdensome, entailing bitter recriminations, bodily injury, expulsion, and even death. The local bishops still retained the obligation to deal with hersey and the Inquisitors always consulted with them and involved them in major decisions. But the birthpangs of a new institution brought stress and misunderstandings which were constantly referred to Rome. Bernard Gui, a distinguished Inquisitor of the following century, described qualities that should characterize an Inquisitor:

> He ought to be diligent and fervent in his zeal for religious truth, the salvation of souls, and the extirpation of heresy. He should so conduct himself amid unpleasant and difficult affairs that he never loses control of himself in fits of temper or anger; nor on the other hand should he give way to debilitating sluggishness and languor, for such torpor saps the vigor of an administrator. The inquistor must be constant, persevering amid dangers and adversities even to death. He should be willing to suffer for the sake of justice, neither rashly precipitating nor shamefully retreating in fear, for such cowardice weakens moral stability. While remaining adamant to the entreaties and blandishments of sinners, nevertheless he must not so harden his heart as to repel appeals to grant delays or to mitigate penances according as circumstances of place and time suggest, for such procedure savors rather of cruelty. By the same token

> he should refrain from too lenient an attitude which degenerates into dissoluteness .... Let him be careful in doubtful cases not to believe too easily everything that appears probable, for such is not always true; nor on the other hand should he stubbornly refuse to believe what may seem improbable, for such is often true. With all diligence, therefore, he should discuss and examine every case and inquire into the truth of the matter .... So let mercy and truth, which should never be far from the mind of the judge, rule his actions and always shine from his face with the result that his judicial decisions never be marred by irregularity nor blemished by avarice or cruelty.[6]

With a few notable exceptions the Friar Inquisitors were punctilious in following the legal code of their office. In this regard it is of more than passing interest to note the opinion of Theodore de Cauzons, himself no apologist for the Inquisition: "The cases of corruption of which we know are very rare, and everything leads us to suppose a general uprightness joined to a rigorous discipline among the inquisitorial personnel."[7]

The Inquisitorial Tribunal in Session.

In all the territory of modern France the number of Inquisitors exercising their office at any one time was quite small, usually two for Languedoc, two for Dauphiné and Provence, and from four to six in the rest of France. The reason for this was that the Inquisitors and their entourage traveled from place to place rather than maintaining a permanent residence in one town. At each sitting the Inquisitor was assisted by two assessors or official witnesses, men chosen for their sound judgement, whose function it was to observe due process and to check on the conduct of the trial. Further, skilled consultants, clerics or laymen, were present to advise the Inquisitor on two main points: were the words and acts of the accused objectively contrary to the Faith and subjectively was the accused really culpable. To these men were referred the names of secret witnesses for evaluation in regard to their disinterestedness and the reliability of their testimony. All this was in accordance with the instructions of Pope Gregory IX:

> When you arrive in a city, summon the bishops, clergy and people, and preach a solemn sermon on faith; then select certain men of good repute to help you in trying the heretics and suspects denounced before your tribunal. All who on examination are found guilty or suspected of heresy must promise to obey absolutely the commands of the church; if they refuse, you must prosecute them, according to the statutes which we have recently promulgated.[8]

The coming of the Inquisitor to a town was announced to the populace-at-large who were summoned to attend a general convocation. In the presence of all the assembled clergy and laity the Inquisitor preached a sermon covering the main truths of the Catholic Faith emphasizing the beliefs that were currently under attack by the heretics. The purpose was to review for all the people the systematic teaching of the Church, to improve their knowledge of the Faith, to answer difficulties that had been raised, and to restore and deepen their Faith. As we have seen, it had always been the attitude of the church that if the faithful received a careful, knowledgeable presentation of the church's teaching on faith and morals they would respond with alacrity. Further, it was felt, that questions raised by the Cathars and the Waldensians that disturbed the faith of the unlearned could easily be settled by the clear explanation of trained theologians. This was the primary mission of the highly trained Friars, the Inquisitors. From all this it was hoped that the properly instructed people would be more secure in their faith, freed from the harmful attacks of the heretics.

In this same spirit of reconciliation, the Inquisitor would then extend a Period of Grace, usually fifteen to thirty days, during which time erring members could of their own volition present themselves before the Inquisitor and abjure their errors. If their wandering from the true faith was not public knowledge, they received only a light, private penance. If, however, their deviation from Catholic teaching was common knowledge, they were given one of the ordinary, lighter canonical penances, e.g., a short pilgrimage, special prayers, fasting, etc.

On the other hand, if the preaching mission did not achieve its goal of strengthening the faith of all the people, then more direct methods were in order to preserve the integrity of the faithful from the harmful incursions of the heretics. Suspects were now summoned to present themselves before the Inquisitor. There they were informed of the suspicions, denunciations and charges that had been laid against them. In the early days of the functioning of the Inquisition, it appears that all the rights of both canon and civil law were accorded to the defense, including the revelation of the names of those levying the charges, and the assistance of a legal advocate, though in practice the aid of a lawyer was frowned upon in consequence of Pope Innocent III's prohibition against attorneys or notaries lending counsel to heretics. Eventually, however, the names of witnesses had to be withheld to protect them from instant retaliation by the family and friends of the accused — a not uncommon occurrence.[9] Also, lawyers had to be removed from the tribunal to prevent their obstreperous conduct from causing the proceedings to degenerate into an adversary exercise.[10]

The Inquisitors preferred to act, rightly or wrongly, on the confessions of the accused, for this precluded the necessity of relying on the testimony of witnesses and on cross examination. Provided the depositions levied against the suspect were well-founded and worthy of serious consideration, the Inquisitor exercised all his persuasive powers to obtain a confession. For full confession constituted sufficient proof for conviction, whereas circumstantial evidence did not.[11] The defendant was promised a lighter sentence if he confessed voluntarily, but if such promises failed to obtain results recourse was had to other measures: imprisonment in close confinement, reduced food, and, later, torture.[12] In lieu of a confession, proof of heresy remained to be established on the testimony of witnesses. Here, too, the inquisitorial tribunal differed from secular trials in that the testimony of criminals, i.e., convicted heretics, was heard, provided the court was convinced of their veracity and disinterestedness. If the evidence was palpably insufficient for conviction, the defendant was able to clear himself through canonical purgation, the number of co-swearers varying according to the seriousness of the suspicion and the dignity of the persons involved.[13] For example, one type of co-swearer would be what is termed today a 'character witness.'

According to the instructions of the pope, the accusations of the witnesses, the declarations of the defendants, the interrogation by the Inquisitors and the responses of the accused, and the decisions reached therefrom, were all to be recorded by notaries in the registers of the inquisitorial tribunal and carefully preserved — as they were. In case of an appeal the register was to be forwarded to Rome.

Interrogations before the inquisitorial tribunal.

A person appearing before the Inquisitor was questioned about any knowledge he might have regarding heresy and heretics, about any association he had had with them, and whether he knew of others who had had such association. He was asked whether he had seen a heretic, where, when, how often and with whom, and about others who were present; whether they had aided them in any way, listened to their preaching or participated in their ceremonies, e.g., the adoration (*melioramentum*), baptism (*consolamentum*), confessions (*servitium*), the blessing of bread, or the kiss of peace. All this information before two witnesses was carefully recorded by a notary, and was cross-checked if that person ever appeared again before the tribunal — as on occasion happened.

In addition to these general questions which were asked of all persons, very specific queries were directed at individuals, as is recorded in the Registers of the Inquisition:[14]

Q. Have you heard anyone say, and have you believed that God was originally one, but that subsequently he was divided into three parts of which one was God the Father, the second the Son and the third the Holy Spirit, and that finally later on these three parts will be reassembled and will become a unity, only one God?

Ans. (*Peter Maury*)[15]

Once when the heretic, Jacques Authié, Peter Montanié, and I were having breakfast, the heretic said: "See how those of the Roman Church beguile you! It is the 'synagogue'! For it teaches men to bless themselves and say: 'In the name of the Father and of the Son and of the Holy Spirit,' as if there were three Gods; nevertheless, there is only one God, my Father."

But I said to him, "Do you not say, you others, that the Son of God descended to the earth to reassemble the sons of Israel, and do you not also make two Gods, the Father and the Son?" He answered me that God the Father and the Son were one. Nevertheless the Father, he said, sent his Son into the world; but when the Son of God returned to his Father, he was one God with the Father, as he had been before. He did not explain to me how the Father and the Son were one before the Father sent the Son into the world, and after he had returned to the Father, nor if the Son was part of God the Father.

I have never heard the heretics say that the Son of God was true God, nor that the Holy Spirit was true God, but only that their Father alone was true God. I myself believed this for about seventeen years. I believed that originally there was one God the Father, who divided into three parts, of which one was himself, who remained always in heaven, the other two were the Son and the Holy Spirit, who descended into the world, sent by the Father, then returned to heaven. And then, by the will of God the Father, there took place a reintegration of God the Father with the Son and the Holy Spirit, and they became one with the Father as they had been originally before the Father was divided into three parts.

Q. Have you heard a heretic say, and have you believed that God the Father was called God the Father, not because he had a natural Son, of the same substance and nature as his own, but only because he had made the spirits and the good souls?

Ans. I have not heard the heretics explain this. But I have heard them say often that they alone, the heretics, were able to say "God our Father," for God is the Father only of the "good men," that is the heretics Perfected; but that he was not God the Father of the "believers" or of anybody else. And this is because God the Father is the God of truth and justice, and for this reason he was the Father of those who are in truth and justice as only the Perfected heretics are, they said. This is why they also said that "believers" and others ought not recite "the Our Father," and that they sinned when they said it, for after a man had said this prayer, he ought not to lie. And when "believers" said it, they lied in calling God their Father since he certainly was not.

Myself, I have never believed the heretics on this point; on the contrary, I have often said "the Our Father."

Q. Have you heard the heretics say, and have you believed that all the good spirits as well as the souls of the angels and of men had been made originally by the good god in heaven, and that there they had sinned and had fallen from heaven, and that some of these spirits had become embodied in human bodies by the bad god?

Ans. I heard the late Jacques Authié, the heretic, say that all the souls of 'the good men,' that is to say the heretics, who were, are, and will be, were made in heaven by God the Father, but then, seduced by the devil in the aforesaid manner [the devil had gotten into heaven disguised as a beautiful woman and had promised the good souls wives, children, sheep, cattle, land and other goods and riches of the lower world] they sinned and fell from heaven into the world of the bad god. When they were there, seeing they had been deceived by the bad god, for he did not fulfill what he had promised, they cried to God the Father to pardon them and to bring them back to heaven. Seeing this, the bad god said that he would give them 'coats' that is to say bodies in which they would forget all the delights which they had had in heaven.

And also the devil made the bodies which are the "coats of forgetting of returning," in which the souls go from coat to coat, that is to say from body to body, until they come to a body where they are saved, because they there have been put into a state of truth and justice, that is to say, they have become heretics. And then, having shed their bodies, they return to heaven. And these spirits go from body to body [reincarnation of souls, metempsychosis] until they are hereticated (i.e., receive the *consolamentum.*)

I have heard a heretic say, concerning the apostle Saint Paul, that his soul had been in thirteen bodies before being able to be saved. He was saved in the last body because he had been put into the state of justice and truth.

But I have never heard the heretics say that all the human spirits, all the souls, had been made by God the Father, or that they had sinned in heaven, but only the spirits or souls which were, are, and will be hereticated (were made by God the Father).

Myself, I believed this, and I remained in this belief for eight years or thereabouts.

Q. Have you heard the heretics say, or did you believe that the spirits and the souls, which came down from heaven, were embodied not only in human bodies but also in the bodies of brute beasts, birds, fish, serpents, toads, and other such animals?

Ans. I have heard some heretics say, particularly Prades Tavernier and William Bélibaste, the deceased heretics, that when the human soul leaves its body, at least from that man who had not been made a 'good Christian,' that is was not a heretic, before his death, this soul enters as quickly as possible into another body, the first body of flesh whatever that it meets, whether that of another man, or that of an animal, or a bird, in order to find rest in that body. In effect, they said, when the soul of a man departed from its body, or the body of an animal, until it has been embodied into another body it will not be able to have rest, for the fire of Satan or the alien god consumes it completely. But when it is incarnated in a body, it has repose and does not suffer from this fire, for the fire is not able to harm it. But when persons have been hereticated before dying, their soul, having left their body, is immediately carried by the angels and archangels to heaven close to God the Father. And, they said, when the bad god saw the soul of the hereticated man rise to heaven, he was extremely angry, and for this reason he makes as much trouble as possible for anyone who wants to be received by the heretics, for after this reception or heretication he no longer had any power over the soul and could not prevent it from returning to heaven.

And, they said, on the one hand the bad god is angered at the heretication of any one, while on the other hand God the Father greatly rejoices, and for this reason "believers" receive great merit before God the Father when they bring all that they can to be hereticated by the heretics.

As for the souls of "believers" who had not been able to be hereticated at their death, they said that after death they were embodied into other bodies, for, they said, no person is able to be saved unless he had become 'a good Christian' that is to say, had been hereticated .... In proof of this embodiment of human souls in the bodies of animals Prades Tavernier and William Bélibaste gave the example of the Cathar who had previously been a horse and had lost a shoe in the mud upon returning to that place now as a man, he found the lost shoe. This is why, too, I have heard heretics say, that since animals may have human souls it is a sin to kill them, or any animal, except rats, snakes and toads.

All this I sometimes believe, at others I do not. I believed it when I was with the heretics, and I doubted it when I thought about it on my own.

Q. Have you heard the heretics say, or have you believed that Christ was truly raised from the dead in the flesh on the third day, or that he was not truly raised, but only in appearance, since he had not really died?

Ans. I have heard the late William Bélibaste, the heretic, say that Christ was not truly raised from the dead, since he was not really dead, but only in appearance.

Q. Have you heard the heretics say, or have you believed that in the holy, catholic and Roman Church there is remission of sins, and that by the faith which it protects and which it preaches there is justification of sinners and growth in virtue, and that there is no salvation outside it?

Ans. I have heard Peter Authié, Prades Tavernier, and Amiel of Perles, deceased heretics, say that there were two churches, the one which pardons and is persecuted, the other which preys upon and flays the people. The former was their church, they said, which was in a state of truth and justice, and it was in it that there was remission of sins, for when one has entered into truth and justice, that is to say, has become a heretic, their church was able to pardon all sins, and salvation can be achieved only in their church. As far as the Roman Church was concerned, it stood for falsehood, and it persecuted 'the good christians,' that is to say, the heretics. In it, they said, there is no remission of sins, nor is any one able to be saved in the faith which it protects and preaches.

And they said that their church had the faith and truth of the Son of God, the holy Apostles Peter and Paul and the other apostles: but that the Roman Church, they said, did not have the faith of the apostles.

Myself, I believed this for about eight years.

Q. Have you heard the heretics say, or have you believed that the baptism given in water to infants and adults in the name of the Father and the Son and the Holy Spirit in the Roman Church was valid for the remission of sins and the reception of grace and for helping to enter the kingdom of heaven, or rather it was the baptism administered by the church of the heretics by the imposition of hands and of the Book?

Ans. I have heard all the heretics say that the baptism administered in the Roman Church in the name of the Father and the Son and the Holy Spirit was absolutely valueless: for the infants since they did not have the used of reason, and also for adults, though they may cement great friendships from god-parents. But in any case it had no value for the remission of sins or for entering the kingdom of heaven.

But the baptism of the heretics, they said, was valid for the remission of all sins, and for entry into the kingdom of heaven. When told how the "believers" committed many serious crimes, they responded that the "believers" were doing wrong, but that all the evil they had done would be remitted when they were received by the heretics. That is why the "believers" relying on this reception committed many evil acts. They said also that a person would not undergo any punishment for these bad acts, after having been received by them, for the good they had accomplished in their other coat (that is to say, in their other body) would be charged to their credit ....

I have heard them say also that much lying occurred when an infant was baptized in the Roman

Church, for when the infants were asked: "What do you wish?" one answered for them: "Faith" when the infant definitely did not ask for it. When the infant was asked: "Do you renounce the devil and all his pomp?" one responded for him: "I do renounce it," when he had done nothing and later would be a sinner. And finally when he is asked: "Do you wish to be baptized?" his god-parent replies for him: "I do wish it." but emphatically the infant does not wish it. On the contrary, he cries and screams, which indicates his displeasure with it. But in the baptism of the heretics no such falsehoods occur.

(*In denying that the ministers of the Roman Church had power to forgive sin*) the heretics claimed that there was no need to confess sins, for all sins were forgiven by the reception of the *consolamentum*. No penance or satisfaction was ever imposed on anyone, for, they said, that any fasting done by the "believers" or anyone else availed nothing toward satisfying for sin, since they were not in the state of truth and justice. The only fasting was done by the Perfected.

On prayer, the heretics said that no "believer" ought to pray to God, for he was not worthy, and especially he ought not to say the "Out Father." Only the Perfected should say this prayer, who were in the state of truth and justice. For when a person says the "Our Father" he ought not lie. They said it was much better to keep silent than to recite the "Our Father."

Q. Have you heard the heretics say, or have you believed that the Body of Christ is in the sacrament on the altar after the words of consecration, or that there is only bread and wine as before the consecration?

Ans. I have heard all the aforesaid heretics say that the body of Christ is not in the sacrament on the altar before or after the consecration, but only bread and wine, for, they said, the Son of God after having seemed to have risen from the dead, told the apostles that henceforth he would not again be put into the hands of sinners, and also that no eyes of flesh would see him. This is why, they said, the body of Christ was not in the hands of priests, and was not able to be seen by eyes of flesh. If on the other hand it was the body of God, he would not allow it to be eaten or to be put in a shameful part of the human body. They said if the body of God was big as the mountain of Morella it would have already been eaten by the priests. They said: "Do you not see, all of you, that when one puts it on the altar it is bread and wine, and it is the same bread and wine before as well as after the priests elevated it?" They mocked the sacrament saying that it had no more virtue or efficacy than ordinary bread and wine.

Myself, when I am with the heretics, I believe this, but afterwards when I am in church and see all the people adoring the consecrated host, I believe then that it is the body of Christ.

Q. Have you heard the heretics say, or have you believed that a marriage between a man and a woman, which is celebrated in the Catholic Church, has no value whatsoever, and that the spouses, when they know each other carnally, sin to the same extent as if they were not married?

Ans. I have heard William Bélibaste and Philip of Coustaussa, deceased heretics, say that a carnal marriage between a man and a woman has no validity .... They said it was always a great sin to know any woman carnally, even one's own wife .... Because the heretics have said that it is an equal sin to know any woman carnally I myself have refrained from marrying or have recourse to any woman for over six years, although I am more than forty years old.

But for "believers," heretics permit marriages between a man and a woman, for they tell their parents: "It is necessary to make certain that good unites with good; if one wishes to do this, it is good; if one does not wish, we ought not to do anything about it." They added also: "It would be well, if God wishes it, that your son takes for his wife a "believing" one, a daughter a "believer," for one ought to plant before his door a good fig tree and not a bad bramble or thorn-bush. A man and a woman ought not to worry about riches in marrying," provided that "believers" are able to marry each other, because then the 'good man' (that is to say a Perfected) many be able to come to them, and if one of them becomes sick, the other will be able to go and bring a heretic to the sick partner so that he may be hereticated.

Q. Did you, at this time, believe that these heretics were good men and spoke the truth, that they had a good faith and a good sect, in which men were able to be saved, and that the doctrine which you heard from them was true, wholly or partially?

Ans. (*Sybille Peyre, a widow*):

I, at the time, thought and believed that these heretics were good people, in that they engaged in great abstinences, never took anything of others, did not render evil for evil, also because they observed chastity. But now I do not hold them to be good people, but on the contrary to be evil, for they are very grasping and selfish, and also because they force people to die "in the *endura.*"[16] But all the doctrines exposed above, all their errors, I believed to be the truth, pressured as I was to believe it. And I remained in this belief for about a year, until they told me not to suckle my daughter, after her heretication, and also because at that time I heard them tell their "believers" to kill those who persecuted them, betrayed them, or denounced them, "for it is necesary to cut down the bad tree" (Matthew VII,19). That is why, since that time, I no longer believed their doctrine to be true, but rather that they were evil people. I provided for them since that time in my house, because I was afraid of them and I loved my husband very much, and I did not wish to offend him. I had observed him to be very attached to these heretics, and Peter Maury was always pressuring him about it.

The decisions of the inquisitorial tribunal.

After the hearing of the accusations and depositions of the witnesses, and the defense of the accused, all the facts of the case were discussed by the Inquisitor and his counsellors. All the evidence, the interrogations and the responses, were permanently recorded in writing, the names of the accusers and witnesses revealed, and the proofs opened for review. Upon reaching a decision in consultation with his advisers the Inquisitor transmitted the records of the trial to the local bishop, and together they agreed on the final sentence. This cooperation between the Inquisitor and the local bishop for some time remained variable and uncertain, and indeed was the object of significant and contrary legislation on the part of succeeding pontiffs during the thirteenth century. Ultimately, in cases where the Inquistor and the local bishop could not agree on an equitable sentence, the entire case was to be referred to Rome in accordance with regular ecclesiastical practice.

Reaction of the populace to the activities of the Inquisition.

As many legislators have learned to their dismay, the mere enacting of laws does not automatically change the cultural and social milieu. This was most emphatically true of the Midi. True, the Count of Toulouse, Raymond VII, and the higher nobility were bound by many prescriptions of the Peace Treaty of Paris, 1229, to root out heresy from their domains. But this change of direction had not filtered down to the villages and the countryside. The same cultural conditions that favored the growth of heresy in the first place still existed, and the reaction to the investigations of the Inquisitors was often hostile, and, at times, violent. A contemporary chronicler, William Pelhisson, aptly recounts the social tensions current in that area:

> "Moreover, in that land in those days Catholics were harassed and in several localities those who searched out heretics were killed, although Lord Raymond, the count, had promised in the treaty of peace that over a period of five years, for every heretic, male or female, he would give two silver marks to the one who seized them and after five years one mark. This happened many times. But the chief men of the region, together with the greater nobles and the burghers and others, protected and hid the heretics. They beat, wounded, and killed those who pursued them, for the prince's entourage was notably corrupted in the faith. And consequently many wicked things were done in the land to the church and to faithful persons."[17]

Thus when the Dominican Inquisitor, William Arnold, in Toulouse cited not only working and artisan class citizens to appear before the tribunal but a number of prominent citizens as well, the latter refused to appear, counting on Raymond VII's support. They insisted that the Inquisitor withdraw his summons. He refused, and as a result the Consuls expelled all the Dominicans from the town, November 1235. The local bishop himself was forced to depart. This violence by the aroused populace was immediately countered by Friar William

Arnold, exiled in neighboring Carcassonne, who forthwith excommunicated the Count and Consuls of Toulouse. Although anyone who attempted to publish this proclamation of the Inquisitor was threatened with death, courageous priests nevertheless announced it in Toulouse and as a result they and the assisting Franciscans were manhandled by the crowds. Pope Gregory IX demanded that Raymond VII restore the Dominicans, which, after some months delay, he did — proclaiming as always his innocence. But the hostility remained.

Similar disturbances and physical violence took place in Narbonne when the Dominican Inquisitor Ferrier in 1234 attempted to carry on his work there. Assisted by some notorious nobles, the local populace and the Consuls took up arms against the Inquisition. The religious issue here served as a convenient excuse for those striving to make political gains, and the king had to intervene.

However sincere and well-intentioned the Inquisitors might be some of their actions were almost bound to rouse vehement reaction, for instance, their posthumous condemnations of deceased heretics followed by exhumations of their corpses and public burnings. On one such occasion in 1234 at Albi, the crowds were so incensed that they roughed-up the Inquisitor and were about to throw him into the Tarn river, when a band of defenders rescued him.[18]

Raymond VII dispatched a long list of complaints to the pope and asked for the removal of the Inquisitors who, he said, were biased against him. Gregory IX granted some of his requests, but did not replace the Inquisitors. Meantime, the pope sent a new papal legate, in 1238, who was empowered to absolve the Count and the Consuls of Toulouse, and to reduce other sentences of the inquisitorial tribunal. All this the new legate proceeded to do. For their part the people of Toulouse simply ignored the Inquisitors. Gregory IX suspended the Inquisition for three months in regard to the men of the Count while they traveled to Rome, and for six months in Toulouse itself. The Inquisitors, discouraged and frustrated by the absolving of the Consuls who had physically mistreated them, were reduced to impotence. Consequently the Dominicans withdrew from the exercise of their mandate — and the suspension continued for three years! Once again the political realities of life made their impact felt: where the civil authorities cooperated, the pope's policies went forward; where they were hostile, the work of the Inquisition ground to a halt.

Political distractions.

On the international scene political upheavals had ripple effects in other areas. In 1237, Frederick II's victory at Cortenuova in Italy wiped out the Lombard League, traditional allies of the papacy in the age-old rivalry between the Ghibellines and the Guelfs. Gregory IX was now faced with a direct threat from the Emperor, who would now command his full attention. Raymond VII was an ally of Frederick II, and it was important for the pope to keep them apart. The implications of this situation were not lost on the Count and his nobles. The Inquisitors were confronted with complete silence from many people, while the Consuls and other officials refused to enforce the civil laws against heresy. Condemned heretics walked the streets of Toulouse in open defiance. Meanwhile, Raymond VII, unmoved by Gregory IX's leniency towards him, joined a league with Henry III of England and the Emperor against Louis IX of France and proceeded to attack the French in Languedoc. Some local nobles, emboldened by the situation , plotted to assassinate the Inquisitors. On the evening of the vigil of the Feast of the Ascension in 1242, the assassins attacked and hacked to death with axes the two Inquisitors, William Arnold, a Dominican Friar, and Stephen of St. Thibéry, a Franciscan Friar, together with nine of their party — the entire group. Retribution was slow in coming, but come it did with the besieging of Montségur, wherein the murderers had taken refuge, by the royal forces under the seneschal of Carcassonne accompanied by local bishops. The town of Montségur was a main headquarters of the Cathars south of Toulouse. After withstanding a siege for over a year, the town surrendered, and the heretics who refused to recant were burned by the king's troops.

The Inquisition to the end of the thirteenth century.

After the death of Gregory IX, who established the Inquisition, the succeeding pontiffs tightened and kept a close surveillance on the proceedings but did not radically change the original tribunal. The Inquisitors themselves, responding to criticisms of their methods of procedure, submitted a number of questions to the bishops assembled at the Council of Narbonne, 1243-44, which was presided over by the legate of Innocent IV. At this Council, and at several others within the next few years, the inquisitorial process was set forth in minute detail:

— an Inquisitor must operate only in his own assigned district.

— no one is to be convicted without sufficient proof or his own confession: "It is better for the guilty to remain unpunished than for the innocent to be punished."

— the different categories of heretics and their supporters are carefully defined:

  — heretics properly so-called are those who publicly persist in their error, e.g., the Perfected.

  — the believers (*credentes*) are those who adhere to the sect but have not yet received the *consolamentum*.

— suspect (*suspectus*) are those who listen to heretical preaching and participate in their liturgy.

— concealers (*celatores*) are those who know heretics but do not denounce them to the authorities.

— hiders (*occutatores*) are those who hide heretics or who thwart attempts to arrest them.

— defenders (*defensores*) are those who take up the defense of heretics in word and in act and seek to neutralize the exercise of the Inquisition.

— supporter (*fautores*) are those who under whatever title give counsel, aid or favor to heretics.

— relapsed (*relapsi*) are those who having once abjured their heresy relapse into their former error.

— in heresy trials, criminals, accomplices, and those branded as canonically 'infamous' are permitted to testify.

— the names of witnesses are not to be published (however the accused is entitled to list the name of his enemies, who then cannot be permitted to testify against him).

— the Inquisitor is to see to it that the accused is provided adequate means to defend himself.

— witnesses are to be protected.

— those who wish to repent are to be absolved and given only light penances.

— if lacking, prisons are to be built.

— the relapsed or the recalcitrant are to be abandoned to the secular arm.

— the Dominican Inquisitors are forbidden to levy fines as punishment, for they as a mendicant Order have the vow of poverty and such procedure could reflect unfavorably on them.

— no attention whatever is to be paid to depositions made out of malice or enmity.

— confiscations are not to be carried out before the accused has been legally convicted.

— the "perfected" of the Cathar heresy who wish to be interrogated in secret may do so in the presence of only a few persons, and if they desire to return to the Church they are to be treated with kindness and given as light a penance as possible.

— those imprisoned for life — in order to give them time to repent and to prevent them from contaminating others — may be released if their family is in grave need.

With the election of Innocent IV (1243-1254), a canon lawyer, a determined effort was made to organize the above mentioned prescriptions and various papal directives into an ordered procedure. A number of "Manuals for Inquisitors" made their appearance, spelling out in precise detail all the legal formalities to be followed:

Letters of Commission, citing the authority and jurisdiction of each Inquisitor.

Methods of Citation, for summoning a general assembly of a parish or a town.

Method of Abjuration, for all persons to forswear all forms of heresy.

Form of Oath, to be taken by all to tell what they knew about heresy and heretics.

Formula of Interrogation, questions to be asked of each person appearing before the tribunal.

Method of Summoning of Individuals, for persons cited by name to appear before the tribunal.

Method and Form of Reconciling and Administering Penances, regarding those who wished to return to the unity of the Faith.

Letters concerning the Performances of Penances, describing in detail such matters as the size and shape of the crosses to be worn, the letters to be notarized by those who have completed their pilgrimages, etc.

The Form of the Sentence for those released to the Secular Arm, the wording of the sentence of the Inquisitor regarding an unrepentant convicted heretic abandoned to the civil government for the application of civil penalties.

Form of the Sentence for those who died as heretics, for exhumation of those buried in consecrated ground.[19]

Pope Innocent IV made it his policy to check the spread of heresy but at the same time to restrain exaggerated persecutions. To this end he prohibited the indiscriminate levying of excommunication and interdict, which forbade all public worship or administration of the Sacraments in a given parish or church. Such action, at times apparently taken hastily by French bishops, had achieved rather the opposite of the effect intended, for, on the one hand, many people protested the harshness of such censures, while on the other hand many persons became accustomed to not fulfilling their religious duties and continued in that vein. The heretics themselves were not affected at all. To remedy this impossible situation the pope ordered his legate to void all such censures inflicted contrary to his instructions.

More positively, in pursuance of his policy of restoring peace to the agitated areas of southern France, Innocent IV took steps to facilitate the return of penitent heretics to the fold. He expanded the privileges of the Period of Grace by authorizing the Inquisitors not only to reconcile those who wished voluntarily to return, but to restore to such all their ecclesiastical rights, without the infliction of any penance whatsoever.

The new legislation, highly organized and less severe, seems to have had a definite affect on actual practice. In the sentences of the Dominican Inquistors Bernard of Caux and John of St. Pierre, 1244 to 1248, there is not recorded a single instance of a person being handed over to the secular arm. However, a flood of appeals against inquisitorial sentences flowed to Rome, and Innocent IV granted many of them. Indeed he suspended, April 21, 1245, the imposing of the most serious penalties, except for manifest heretics, until the holding of the Council of Lyons. These actions of the pope in turn created turmoil in the operation of the Inquisition, and a number of bishops protested to him that the Dominicans were innocent of the charges levied against them and were so frustrated that all faith and discipline were being brought into disrepute, including the authority of the pope himself. While the Inquisition seems to have continued sporadically, it was on a very reduced scale. A cleric and a courier were murdered at Caunes in 1247 and the inquisitorial registers burned. Raymond VII complained that the reduced activity encouraged the growth of heresy. Two of the Dominican Inquisitors simply quit, and the Dominican Chapter held in Paris asked the pope to permit the Dominicans of Provence to withdraw entirely because of this extremely dangerous situation.

Innocent IV declined to accede to this request. The matter came to a head when 156 citizens of Limoux appealed to Rome against the sentences of the Inquisitor. Innocent IV instructed the Prior of Prouille to annul the sentences and give lesser ones. The Inquisitor simply removed all penalties. A serious impasse had arisen between the pope and the Inquisitors. On this occasion the pope had to annul his own annulments.[20]

Innocent IV and the Dominican Inquistors.

The Inquisitors felt completely frustrated by the continuing practice of the pope in hearing and granting numerous appeals against their decisions — and they simply withdrew. Innocent IV did not intend to abdicate his authority and he continued regularly to authorize local bishops and his own personal legate to reduce and commute sentences of the Inquisitors. Further, he criticized the Inquisitors for having too many assistants and for incurring too heavy expenses. Not that the Inquisition as such ceased to function, rather the pope began to rely more and more on the local bishops to carry on this work — and they did, appointing their own diocesan priests as Inquisitors. After some years it appears that all concerned had grown weary of this burdensome task and would have liked nothing more than that the Dominicans would once more resume their inquisitorial duties. Alphonse, brother of the king and now Count of Toulouse, tried to induce them to do so. Innocent IV ordered the Dominican Provincial of Provence to appoint Inquisitors — but they would have none of it. In 1252 the bishops of Toulouse, Agen, Albi, and Carpentras addressed a collective letter to the Dominicans to the same purpose, promising that they would not interfere with their sentences provided that they were levied in canonical form. But they answered with impenetrable silence! After several other fruitless attempts by Innocent IV to gain the support of the Dominicans, he in 1254 asked the Franciscans to send Inquisitors into Toulouse. But the impasse remained until his death.

The Inquisition under the Dominicans resumes.

Upon assumption of office Pope Alexander IV (1254-1261) renewed efforts to obtain the support of both the Dominicans and the Franciscans — but with no noticeable result. Only in 1258/59 does it become evident that the Friar Inquisitors have resumed their normal activities, with full papal support. Evidently the point had been made and the Dominicans felt that they now could perform their office without undue interference. From this time forward until the end of the century the inquisitorial tribunal functioned in a normal manner, without reference to the crisis under Innocent IV. There were no new Councils or special papal legates. Alexander IV instructed the Dominican Inquisitors to take control over the inquisitorial registers, to reconcile those who wished to return to the fold, to investigate heretics in whatever jurisdiction they may have fled from Toulouse, but admonished them to follow the order of procedure laid down by the preceding Councils. He himself settled disputed points but left the ordinary operation of the Inquisition to the Inquisitors themselves — and supported their efforts.

There were no other significant changes in the inquisitorial procedure by the popes through the end of the thirteenth century. Pope Boniface VIII (1294-1303), a canon lawyer, codified previous papal and conciliar regulations and inserted them in the official collection of Canon Law, the *Corpus juris canonici.*[21] He did provide additional safeguards for the protection of defendants in that he decreed that both the bishop and the Inquisitor must reciprocally reveal to each other the names of the accusers and the witnesses; in heresy trials reliable persons skilled in the law should be called in to hear all the evidence and to assist in an official capacity the Inquisitor in rendering his decisions; under pledge of secrecy the names of the accusers and the witnesses should be revealed to these *jurisperiti.* But once the grave danger had passed on account of which the names had been kept secret they then must be revealed forthwith not only to the *boni viri,* but especially to the accused themselves.[22]

These, then, are the main features of the Inquisition as it functioned in the thirteenth century in southern France. The inquisitorial tribunal was a court of exception designed to deal with an urgent situation created by the impact of the Albigensian and Waldensian heresies. For the first time a special court was established to weigh the evidence presented and to adjudicate the charges according to law. Moreover the Inquisitor was empowered to seek out the evidence and present it, much as our District Attorneys do today. Certain particular aspects of the inquisitorial process have caused controversy down through the years. The following Chapter addresses them.

CHAPTER IV
CONTROVERSIAL ASPECTS OF THE INQUISITORIAL TRIBUNAL

It is the inescapable responsibility of the historian to recreate the atmosphere of a different era to such an extent that a present-day reader may comprehend the conditions that governed men's attitudes during that period: to explain, not to excuse. Failing this, no author can hope to portray a truthful picture of a past culture; much less may a modern reader,without it, pretend to understand the actions of his forebears. Where religious and juridical practices were so radically at variance with modern ways, as were surely those of the thirteenth century, a major effort is called for. On the one hand, heresy was primarily and essentially a religious issue, while, on the other, the method of ascertaining whether a person was actually a heretic or not was a juridical task.

In the high Middle Ages, Christendom encompassed all the feudal States of Europe, whose citizens were all Christian:

> "The same faith was the common heritage of high and low alike, on the banks of the Danube, Rhine, or Rhone, or Thames .... Christianity was included in the very definition of their citizenship .... By heresy, they sinned against the citizenship in which all shared. The strength of this feeling goes a long way to explain that the first violence done against the heretics, the first lynchings, were the work not of the rulers, ecclesiastic or temporal, but of the common people - a spontaneous outburst against what outraged their deepest instincts. It was a symptom of the close interlocking of Church and State, whatever other factors were involved.[1]"

In order to bring some semblance of order out of heedless mob action it was of first importance to determine the exact beliefs and practices of the major dissident sects - the

Cathars and the Waldensians - and the supporting reasons why they so believed.[2] These doctrines were then compared with the teachings of the Roman Church, for both groups claimed that they were the true Christians trying to recapture the original, the pristine faith of the church, the faith of the Apostles. To the extent that their creeds were found to differ from the Catholic Church, the new movements were termed heretical. The purpose of the investigation, the *'inquisitio,'* was to point out to the dissenters wherein their teachings strayed from that of the Roman Church and, hopefully, to win them back to their former allegiance. If a wayward son or daughter acknowledged his/her error and was received back into full communion with the Church, success was achieved. A salutary penance was given to the penitent - as is done today in the Sacrament of Penance. On the other hand, if the person knowingly and adamantly persisted in his/her heterodox beliefs, the Church then sorrowfully acknowledged defeat, solemnly declared the person a heretic, removed him/her from the communion of the faithful, and handed him/her over to the Secular Power to answer for the crime of disloyalty committed against political society. In this way the faithful were protected from the contagion of evil doctrine, and the State preserved the integrity of the political and social order. For in the thirteenth century, and long before, Church and State worked closely together to protect and maintain the religious, social, and political stability that all believed necessary for the commonweal. In principle the separation of Church and State was insisted upon, even though the close interdependence of one on the other brought them into continuous association. The Church became heavily entangled in the feudal system, so much so that its ministers, even bishops, were chosen by the State and its property handled at times as a private possession by lay expropriators. It was only a mighty effort by the Gregorian Reform that reversed this stranglehold. The State in its turn had depended enormously on the Church for its legitimacy, for its higher trained officials and for the only education and culture that existed. Therefore, the unity of Christendom was sundered not only by the anti-ecclesiastical attitude of these new heretical sects, but by their anti-social nature as well (marriage was evil, all oaths upon which feudalism depended were prohibited, the coërcive power of political authorities was denied - all of which undermined the very existence of organized society). In the twentieth century this kind of correlation and consensus simply does not exist.

As the question of creeds was a religious one, so the procedure utilized to determine whether one was a heretic or not was juridic, and its validity can only be rationally discussed against the background of thirteenth century law, canonical and civil. For here again Church and State legal practice mutually influenced each other. Since this is an historical fact, it is necessary to view it in its historical setting. The main points that are of particular interest to the present-day reader are the following:

1. The inquisition itself as a method of juridic process.

2. Secrecy in regard to the names of witnesses.

3. The presence, or lack thereof, of a defense lawyer.

4. The methods of proof: ordeals - oaths - torture.

1. *The Inquisition itself as a method of juridic process.*

One of the glories of the Roman Empire, which the Middle Ages admired and sought to use to advantage, was the brilliant codification of Roman Law, the *Corpus juris civilis.* It greatly influenced both canon (Church) law and civil law in the Middle Ages. It was just in these centuries that it was being revived, and called the Reception of Roman Law. Much of the current thirteenth century trial procedure had its origin in Roman Law. The three methods of trial known at the time were termed the 'accusation,' the 'denunciation,' and the 'inquisition.' The accusatory was the ordinary method; the other two, extraordinary.[3]

A. *Accusation (accusatio).*

In the time of the Roman Republic and during the Empire and the Middle Ages, the ordinary way of bringing an alleged criminal to justice was by way of a private accusation to a magistrate or judge or feudal lord. It was regarded as a private affair, and not the function of public officials - there was no such person as a district attorney or a public prosecutor. The plaintiff then had to prove his charge against the accused before the judge, who merely acted as a kind of referee between the two parties. Among other difficulties of this procedure was the intimidating presence of the wealthy or powerful on the one hand, and the time lost and the embarrassment of persons, e.g., bishops, in standing trial against frivolous and malicious accusations. To remedy this abuse, the law of retaliation, the *lex talionis*, was added to the requirement of laying an accusation, to wit, that if the plaintiff could not prove his charge, then he himself had to suffer the consequences prescribed for the crime he had unsuccessfully charge another with. Needless to say, this had a dampening affect on future accusations; and too often criminals went free, with no one to bring them to justice.[4]

B. *Denunciation (denunciatio).*

In the second method, a private individual made known to legitimate authority a crime, without assuming responsibility for proving the accusation. The charge had to be in writing, stating the name of the accuser and of the accused, together with all the circumstances and proofs available. It was then up to the judge to act on the information or not.

C. *Inquisition (inquisitio).*

The third method consisted of an investigation made of a crime or criminal activity by a legitimate judge. The deficiencies of the first two methods were obvious; 1) the fear of having to undergo the penalty attached to the crime one had charged another with, unsuccessfully, the *poena talionis;* 2) the very real danger of mutilation or death in the trial by combat with the accused; 3) the necessity of inflicting the penalty on the guilty party by the one who had successfully brought the charge; 4) the fact that both the 'accusatory' and the 'denunciatory' procedures were private affairs, so that the duty to act against crime too often slumbered in inactivity, fear, lethargy - and crime went unpunished. What was needed was an official charged with the obligation of investigating and dealing juridically with criminal activities. The other methods of private, popular accusation, the *actio popularis* so dear to Roman tradition (indeed the Romans never conceived of a public official whose office it would be to prosecute in the name of society) had been tried in both Roman Law and Conciliar Decrees with but indifferent success.

Pope Innocent III (1198-1216), himself a canon lawyer, was dissatisfied with the patent inadequacies of the previous crude forms of procedure. In the legislation he proposed for consideration at the Fourth Lateran Council in 1215, Innocent improved on and promoted the 'inquisition' - the *enquête,* the inquiry - as the ordinary method to be adopted in ecclesiastical trials. So well was it eventually received that its use spread throughout the courts of Europe and became the prevailing system in secular courts for centuries. Canon Six of the Fourth Lateran Council provided for the appointment of permanent officials, synodal witnesses, to investigate clerical abuses in a diocese and to report their findings to the bishop for action. This was the 'general inquisition' to remedy delinquencies in a diocese. Canon Eight of the Council, on the other hand, instituted the 'special inquisition' wherein the judge lays aside his traditional role of an impartial arbiter and now actually conducts an investigation of crime in virtue of his office. The Council empowered him to arrest, cite, produce witnesses, admit or reject proofs, examine the prisoner and, should the evidence warrant it, condemn the guilty, e.g., remove him from office. And interestingly enough, all this was designed, not for heresy, but to investigate and adjudicate delinquencies among the *clergy itself!*

This concise, closely reasoned legislation comprises a summary of the historical development of law together with the new decrees intended to remedy the shortcomings of the 'accusatory' and 'denunciatory' methods. However, the movement towards giving the judge more authority to conduct the trial ran counter to the popular prejudice of law that one man should not be both the accuser and the judge. The Church as yet did not envisage an official prosecution, as a public prosecutor did not exist.[5] Canon Eight, as noted above, legally removed this hindrance by providing that when repeated complaints of serious delinquencies by bishops and clerics reach the ears of a superior church official, "not indeed from spiteful and slanderous persons, but from those who are prudent and upright persons" [it was because of such slanderous libels in the past that a previous Council had added the *poena talionis* to the prevailing 'accusatory' procedure] he was then empowered to investigate, try, and punish, for in such circumstances the 'accuser' is, not the judge, but the 'public ill-fame' surrounding the accused. Because of the verified notoriety of the person in question, he became in law *'infamatus'* (*infamous*); his 'infamy' then took the place of an accuser, while the judge's impartiality remained intact. This new procedure was in accord with a current practice based on Roman ideas which had the judge lead the inquiry, conduct the trial, and pronounce the judgement.

Thus Innocent III, while ever conscious of the popular distaste for the same man being both accuser and judge, went along with the legal fiction of permitting 'the public outrage' to be sufficient for summoning a person to an accounting. But this was only a halfway measure that really did not solve the problem of bringing notorious persons to the bar. For once the popular clamor or the synodal witness had brought the person to court, they then withdrew; they had no part in the examination of the accused. It still seemed as if the judge and the accuser were the same, despite this legal fiction. What was needed was for the synodal witness, who according to Canon Six of the Council, was to investigate the evil report and notify the bishop, to continue on as an active participant in the trial.

This step, however, would not be taken until a score of years later when the 'inquisitorial procedure' was adapted by Pope Gregory IX (1227-1241) as a specific institution (the Inquisition) to deal with heresy. As the Inquisitor under the new mandate from Gregory IX organized the process for investigating heresy and heretics, he found it advantageous to appoint minor officials to make the original inquiries and then to assist him in the actual process of the trial. Out of this practice grew the office of 'minister of the inquisition,' who was really basically concerned with the investigation of heresy and with prosecuting the accused before the inquisitorial tribunal itself. From this auxiliary office developed the Promoter of Justice in church courts, whose duty it was to investigate wrong doing and to prosecute offenders. In this same century emerged the French office of *procurateur de roi*, and eventually states' attorneys, precursors of modern day district attorneys.

Thus the Church substituted the inquisitorial procedure for the defective accusatory process. A rational inquiry was now introduced as the ordinary method of weighing the evidence and of deciding the guilt or innocence of an accused person. Moreover a designated official now assumed the responsibility for investigating and prosecuting alleged offenders. Both of these developments found their way into the legal systems of continental Europe. Indeed the *'enquête'* of Louis IX of France is one of the glories of his reign, and a milestone in legal history. The inquisitorial procedure owes its modern day reputation to its association with the tribunal of the Inquisition, with which it has been mistakenly identified.[6]

2. *Secrecy in regard to the names of witnesses.*

The inquisitorial procedure, then, was designed to remedy the deficiencies of the traditional accusatory method which made the detection and prosecution of criminal offenses dependent upon private initiative. The inquisition evolved by the Church to deal more effectively with abuses by the clergy was shortly adapted as a special agency in response to the exigencies engendered by the growth and spread of heresy. The Inquisition as an institution as well as a legal method of procedure was a court of exception, of extraordinary and summary procedure, in the face of a virulent and pressing danger. As one canon lawyer has put it:

> "The object of the summary trial is to make the canonical process shorter, not to abolish it. Hence it would be a mistake to suppose that in this process the proceedings could be less thorough, less complete, or less exhaustive, or that the proofs could be less perfect or less full than in a formal trial. No difference exists in this respect between the summary and formal trials."[7]

Even circumscribed as it was with various legal restrictions in regard to the defense of the accused, it established definite rules for gathering and sifting evidence and provided a specially delegated prosecutor and judge to pass on the testimony so presented.

In the early days of the operation of the Inquisition as organized by Gregory IX, it would appear that all the rights of canon and civil law were guaranteed to the defense, including the revelation of the names of those bringing the charges. This was standard procedure.[8] But as the history of legal processes testifies over and over again - as we have already seen in the change from accusatory to inquisitorial procedures - the actual functioning of the operating machinery had to be modified by the realities of circumstances. Thus, upon arraignment the accused was informed of the suspicions, denunciations and charges levied against him. With the growth and extension of the operations of the Inquisitors and the experience gained thereby, it became increasingly evident that some protection must be afforded the witnesses, else no one could be prevailed upon to testify. So high did feelings run in the Midi, so widespread was the heresy involved, that vengeance was apt to be sure and fast. One well-known authority described the situation quite baldly:

> "Although [harm to the interests of the accused] so resulted in certain cases, the inquisitorial custom of which we are speaking had not been invented to hinder the defense of the accused; it was born of the special circumstances in which the inquisition was founded. The witnesses, the denouncers of heretics, had had to suffer for their deposition before the judges: many had disappeared, stabbed or thrown into the ravines of the mountains by the relatives, friends, or co-religionists of the accused. It was this danger of bloody reprisals which caused the law of which we are speaking to be imposed. Without it, neither the accusers nor the witnesses would have desired to risk their lives and to depose before the tribunal at that price; it was necessary in order to protect them and to make them talk to promise them inviolable secrecy."[9]

Add to this that a never too effective civil administration had been disrupted by a long, bitter crusade and by subsequent disorder, and the precarious situation of unpopular witnesses becomes apparent. That the witnesses were in imminent peril is an historical fact, and both ecclesiastical and lay courts so recognized it.[10] Because, then, of the attendant dangers to prospective witnesses, twenty years after Gregory IX instituted the Inquisition, at the request of the Inquisitors Pope Innocent IV in 1254 withdrew this privilege and authorized the withholding of the names of witnesses. He stated at the same time, however, that the names must be revealed to the assessors or *jurisperiti,* discreet and honorable experts who sat with the Inquisitor. It was their duty to evaluate the disinterestedness and reliability of the secret witnesses. In order to overcome the obvious hindrance to the defense, the accused was permitted to name his enemies or those who might wish to harm him, and their testimony was prohibited. Further, the various councillors and *boni viri* who were part of the tribunal were bound to report all arbitrary decisions and abuses of the Inquisitor to the local bishop, his religious superiors, and even to the Roman Pontiff himself - which on occasion happened. Even though the special inquisitorial tribunal was permitted to withhold the names of witnesses, the depositions themselves were always written down and a copy given to the accused. Early in the next century Pope Boniface VIII decreed that when the danger had passed the names must be revealed to the accused, and he saw to it that his orders were obeyed. In the current French practice of the thirteenth century King Louis IX also forbade the publication of the names of witnesses in civil criminal trials - and for the same reasons. But later on in the century by the Ordonnance of 1276 not only the names of the witnesses but even their depositions were denied to the accused.[11]

Twentieth century United States with all its strict and tightly organized administration, its courts and police, and its Federal Bureau of Investigation is not immune from the same problem: the safety of witnesses. Henry Hill, a witness in a basketball point-shaving case, is currently in the Federal Witness Protection Program (New York TIMES 1/18/1981); as also are: Ralph Picardo, a witness in labor racketeering cases (New York TIMES 1/18/1981); Judy Wicks, since receiving death threats (Washington POST 1/17/1981); and Joe Teitelbaum, living and working in Miami in the shipping business under his own name, but with a round-the-clock bodyguard of federal marshals who seem to resent his unwillingness to assume a false identity and relocate. After all, his protection is costing the government $4,000 a day! The examples are endless!

3. *The presence, or lack, of a defense lawyer.*

Another departure from the ordinary practice of ecclesiastical and civil courts was the eventual prohibition, for a time, of the assistance of a lawyer for the accused before the inquisitorial tribunal. Originally, the suspect was granted all the rights of canon and civil law, which included the counsel of an attorney. Pope Innocent III in an attempt to eliminate any sort of approval of or encouragement to heretics had frowned upon any recourse to heretical lawyers for legal work:

> "If he [a heretic] be an advocate, let his assistance by no means be sought."[12]

From this admonition the idea grew, by the labyrinthian reasoning that only lawyers can devise, that a heretic before the inquisitorial tribunal should not have a lawyer. This attitude was maintained by Gregory IX and Innocent IV, but legal advocates were not formally barred. Lawyers were finally forbidden to heretics, however, by Pope Urban IV (1261-1264), a prohibition which was withdrawn in the fourteenth century.

The reasons for this restriction seems initially to have stemmed not only from Innocent III's intention to restrain the spread of heresy, but also, in this court of exception, to discourage the histrionics and dilatory tactics of lawyers which might turn the whole proceedings into an adversary process. Several contemporary Church Councils in Languedoc had officially complained about this abuse. The whole process was to save, not to condemn, the suspect - however drastic the eventual outcome might be. The phrase used by Pope Urban IV and succeeding popes down to the fourteenth century was that trials in this court were to be conducted simply and without the verbosity and tergiversations of advocates and lawyers: "*simpliciter et de plano ac sine strepitu et figura judicii.*" As in many legal wranglings, this phrase itself raised more questions than it settled, and finally Pope Clement V's clarifying definition was adopted by the Council of Vienne in 1311:

> "It often happens that we commit causes and in some of them we order that the cause proceed *simpliciter et de plano, ac sine strepitu et figura judicii.* The meaning of these words is disputed by many and they doubt how to proceed. We, desiring to settle this doubt .... approve by this constitution which shall forever obtain in the future, that the judge to whom such a cause is committed, need not necessarily demand a libellus, nor the joiner of issues, in order to proceed, on account of necessity, also on ferial days. Let him shorten delays, let him make the trial brief in so far as he can by repelling exceptions, dilatory and vain appeals, by restraining the disputes and quarrels of the advocates and the procurators and a superfluous multitude of witnesses.[13]"

In the secular realm Emperor Frederick II had prohibited lawyers in such cases since 1220. However cogent the reasons for this prohibition may seem to have been for the papacy in the latter thirteenth century, it was removed in the next.[14]

4. *The methods of proof: ordeals - oaths - torture.*

A distinguished international authority on the history of law, echoing the teachings of all legal historians, has summarized the development of legal procedure from feudal times through the 1200s - the period with which we are concerned - down to the twentieth century:

> "The public prosecution of a suspected criminal before the law courts is an indispensable feature of modern

society: as soon as sufficient evidence is available the grand jury or the director of public prosecutions formally incriminates the suspect and the trial ensues, to establish his guilt or innocence, to condemn or acquit. Private complaint by the victim or his relatives plays a minor role in present day criminal procedure. This used not to be the case and public prosecution, as we know it, is the product of a long development. Originally most criminal offenses were considered as violations of private rights and led to extra-judicial vengeance or compensation. With the emergence of law courts and the judicial settling of claims, the need arose for a formal complaint to set the criminal plea in motion (except when the criminal was taken in the act and summarily dealt with). For centuries the right to bring this complaint belonged to a private person and the criminal plea was a contest, where accuser and accused fought on an equal footing under the formal guidance of the court; they fought with oaths, sworn by themselves and their oath-helpers (foreoaths and purgatory oaths), with sticks or swords in judicial combat, or with other primitive modes of proof. Both parties ran heavy risks: at worst, the accuser who failed to prove his case might undergo the punishment he had hoped to obtain for his opponent (unless he had already fallen in judicial combat); at best he would suffer some minor penalty. Leaving the impleading of criminals to the uncertain and very risky initiative of private avengers was quite inadequate for the defense of public order, and led, with the emergence of modern ideas about the state, to the replacement of the accusatorial by the inquisitorial procedure. Then the prosecution of crime was entrusted to an official organ, proceeding *ex officio*, and purgatory oaths and ordeals were replaced by modern means of inquiry. This transition is a common European phenomenon and, without belittling the attempts of the Carolingian

> monarchy, it may safely be considered a product of the emergence, from the twelfth century onwards, of the centralized state."[15]

But the transition took time. Old customs die not easily, and the judicial duel remained legal in royal courts for capital punishment cases well into the reign of Philip the Fair, King of France, in the fourteenth century.

Methods of proof of guilt or innocence: ordeals - trial by combat.

It was one thing to bring a suspect before a judge; it was quite another to establish his guilt or innocence. In the Middle Ages with the decentralization of government, justice was administered by hundreds of independent feudal barons, counts, lords; it was local, crude, weak, selfish. In such circumstances people could not see why a judge, a man like themselves, should have superior power to declare them guilty of a crime. This difficulty was overcome by an appeal to God for adjudication. It appears that Germanic tribes had adopted a number of trials, particularly of personal combat, to determine justice in a dispute. With their conversion to Christianity it came but naturally to their minds to use these and other trials to appeal directly to God to make known His decision. The people of the Middle Ages believed firmly in God and were quite willing to accept His judgement in criminal cases. Thus the facts of the case, undetermined, were superceded by "the judgment of God," the ordeals.

Ordeals[16] were a means of determining the guilt or innocence of an accused person by an appeal to the direct intervention of God. The main barbarian ordeals were trial by combat, the judicial duel, and the trial by lots. In the judicial duel the accuser and the accused fought each other in deadly combat with swords, spears, or whatever, confident that God would give victory to the innocent. As this non-rational (i.e., the pros and cons of the actual evidence were not weighed) method of determining guilt spread to the Christian faithful, more religious ideas found their way into various types of ordeals:

Trial of the Eucharist: the accused would be induced to receive Holy Communion in the belief that, if he was guilty, God would punish him with instant death.

Trial of the cross: both parties, the accuser and the accused, would stand before a cross with their arms outstretched. The first one to drop his arms was defeated and, therefore, presumed guilty.

Trial by hot water: the accused would draw a stone from the bottom of a boiling cauldron. His hand was bandaged and if after three days his hand was found to be sound, he was acquitted.

Trial by cold water: the accused would be bound hand and foot and lowered into the water. If he sank, he was deemed innocent; if he floated, he was considered guilty - on the belief that water being pure would expel anything impure put into it.[17]

Trial by judicial combat: the accuser and the accused, or their representatives, would fight in mortal combat, i.e., until one or other was slain. The victor was assumed to be the innocent party.

However sincere the faithful were in their belief in God's supernatural intervention in ordeals, it was scarcely a reasonable way for determining guilt or innocence. In fact its use could become increasingly injurious when, for instance, it might be thought that the surest way to win in a judical combat was to hire the best champion to represent oneself; or when, as one chronicler tells us, a man carefully tested his three sons to see which was best at holding his breath and therefore the one most likely to be successful in an impending cold water trial. In any case, Pope Innocent III effectively put a stop to this procedure in Canon Eighteen of the Fourth Lateran Council in 1215:[18]

> "Neither shall anyone [cleric] in judicial tests or ordeals by hot or cold water bestow any blessing; the earlier prohibitions in regard to dueling remain in force."

All well and good, but the courts were placed in a serious dilemma: how now was the guilt or innocence of an accused person to be determined?

Methods of proof of guilt or innocence: compurgation - the taking of oaths and oath helpers.

The other method of clearing one's name from an accusation was purgation, achieved by the taking of an oath: an invocation of the Divine Name, calling on God to witness to an assertion as being true.

> "Undoubtedly, the intrinsic value of the oath arises from its deeply religious character and significance. The oath is an acknowledgement by man of God's infinite truth, knowledge and justice. It is an attempt to take man's judgment out of the sphere of the natural and the temporal and to place it in the realm of the supernatural and the eternal. He who takes the oath assumes a most serious responsibility. He places his testimony in the hands of God Himself, Whose all-comprehensive knowledge will discern and Whose unfailing justice will punish, in time or in eternity, any deliberate falsehood which shall pass his lips."[19]

Of old the prophet Jeremiah had laid down the requirements for the taking of a lawful oath. "And thou shalt swear: As the

Lord liveth, in truth, and in judgment and in justice ..." (Jeremiah IV,2). One swears to tell the truth; there is a serious reason for taking this oath; the matter about which one swears is lawful. All courts of law have utilized oaths to preserve their integrity and to secure justice. This was most especially true of the feudal system which relied on it almost exclusively for welding together the body politic. This was central to one of the grave difficulties posed by the Albigensians and the Waldensians: they refused to take any oaths for any reason whatsoever, based on their interpretation of the New Testament passage: "But I tell you this: You are not to swear at all" (Matthew V,34), and by their own peculiar exegesis, they extended this prohibition to the denial of the right of the State to exercise criminal jurisdiction.

The swelling numbers of Germanic tribes bursting through the territories of the crumbling Roman Empire brought with them the custom of compurgation in criminal trials, as expressed in their own laws modeled on the Roman Codes. Fundamental to the practice of Germanic law was a firm belief in an all-knowing, all-powerful personal God Who was fully aware of all that was going on in this world. Being a God of justice, He would protect the innocent from unjust accusations and would work a miracle, if need be, to defend him, while on the other hand the guilty would suffer divine retribution wherever he might flee. Further, the primitive political organization was tribal, not territorial, which meant that tribal law followed a person wherever he might be - in contrast to Roman Law, which was territorial and bound everyone within the political boundaries. In Teutonic courts, then, blood relationship among members of the clan was emphasized, and the judge relied heavily on relatives and friends of the contending parties to substantiate their honesty and integrity.

In criminal trials, then, after the accused and the accuser had argued their case before the judge, he would decide which one would have to be "the proving party." In most cases this would be the defendant. He could call witnesses to give sworn testimony as to the facts of the case. More commonly, "the proving party" swore to the truth of his own testimony and called upon a number of his relatives and friends to swear as to his honesty and integrity - modern day "character witnesses." The number of the "oath takers" depended upon the nature of the offense and the dignity of the individual. Sometimes they were referred to as "the hand," hence seven oath takers were referred to as "the seventh hand." If "the proving party" and his witnesses and oath takers refuted all the charges, the judge had to render a verdict in his favor. If not, then the ultimate proof would rest upon the result of the ordeal which "the proving party" would have to undergo.

The Church never looked with favor on the so-called "common purgation," i.e., ordeals, and has specifically forbidden judicial duels long since. The early popes termed them "temptation of God" and "superstitious inventions"; but they were supported by individual bishops and prelates, and Charlemagne was enthusiastic about their use. However the Church did make extensive use of "canonical purgation," the taking of an oath as to one's innocence, and the summoning of co-swearers regarding the integrity and reliability of the accused. It was employed when the charges against a person remained unproven, and was considered a supplementary proof. Thus when a bishop was charged with a serious offense and conclusive proof was lacking, he could be ordered to purge himself by taking an oath that he was telling the truth, and provide a number of bishops or abbots to swear that he was worthy of belief.

However, the above methods of proof in criminal trials, the giving of oaths as well as undergoing ordeals, were essentially non-rational, and really did not assist in resolving the facts of the case, if both parties swore to contradictories. Pope Innocent III's prohibition of clerical participation in ordeals spelt the end of this system, but the establishing of a new one was not quite so peremptory.

The question at issue required a whole change of perspective in regard to crime. It could no longer be viewed as a personal offense between two private individuals but rather as a public crime inimical to the peace and tranquillity of the commonweal. Therefore it should be the prerogative of the body politic to investigate, hold trial and punish. This presupposed a centralized government which would organize competent personnel to perform these functions. A very large step was taken by the Church in elaborating the trial by investigation, *per inquisitionem,* the *enquête,* in which the pros and cons of the matter were weighed in court and the case decided on the basis of the evidence presented. Originally the Inquisitor relied on the popular clamor, the hue and cry, the notoriety of the individual to bring the person to the official attention of the judge. But with the organization of the inquisitorial tribunal the Inquisitor gradually employed separate officials to investigate offenses, and, to present the evidence in court, the "minister of the inquisition."

But a third factor remained as a major stumbling block: what kind of proof would be sufficient for conviction. Legal processes are not born full grown out of the sea like Venus, but rather are the result of a continuous evolution. While the people of the Middle Ages, the Ages of Faith, were quite willing to accept the "judgment of God," the ordeals, they were hard put to see why another man like themselves should have the superior power of judging them. And so, the determining factor in devising a new rational system of proofs, i.e., one based on objective evidence, was once again the Roman ideal of law. The decision in a criminal case must be based on objective, certain evidence, entirely independent of the will of a judge, which could be subjective and arbitrary. The judge was to be circumscribed by the ancient Roman tradition of complete, full proof, without which an accused could not be convicted of a capital offense. The Roman-canon law of proof governed judicial procedure in capital cases in the High Middle Ages and well into modern times:

1. The testimony of two eye witnesses was sufficient for conviction and constituted full proof.

2. The confession of the accused was accepted as full proof.

3. Circumstantial evidence, however compelling, was insufficient for conviction in a capital case.

This system of statutory objective proof was intended to protect the accused against the subjective, arbitrary judgment of the judge. The accused could only be convicted on objective criteria; the judge could merely certify that statutory proofs were present, that there were two eye witnesses, or that a full confession had been made. Anything less than full proof was regarded as no proof at all, and hence no conviction. Thus the evidence must be clear as the light of day; there must be no shadow of doubt. This presumably guaranteed absolute justice.

But while solving one problem, the jurists had created another. The demands for "full proof" made conviction for capital crimes most difficult. The two eye witnesses dictum was hard to tamper with, but the confession rule was open to pressure. It was obvious that unobserved major crimes could not be permitted to escape unpunished. But the emphasis on voluntary confession, according to the legal axiom, "confession is the queen of proofs," led to a fateful step, the *introduction of torture.* As one of the distinguished professors of law has put it:

> "To go from accepting a voluntary confession to coercing a confession from someone against whom there was already strong suspicion was a relatively small step .... Actually, judicial torture may not have seemed to contemporaries to be very far from the ordeals. Both were physically discomforting modes of procedure ordered by the court upon a preliminary

> showing of cogent incriminating evidence, usually circumstantial evidence. In this sense, the ordeals may have helped suggest and legitimate the system of judicial torture that displaced them."[20]

Even here, the objective, even-handed principles of Roman-canon law attempted to lay down predetermined standards for evaluating the items of circumstantial evidence. To each item was assigned a numerical value: full proof, half proof, quarter proof, and presumptions - thus limiting judicial discretion. Hence, circumstantial evidence was introduced, not to convict, but only to justify the use of torture. Full proofs, as we have seen, were but two: two eye witnesses, or a confession. Half proof might be one eye witness, or one who saw the accused running from the scene of the crime. Quarter proof might be a bloody axe in the hands of the accused, or blood on his clothes. A number of safeguards were established which had to be verified before the judge could order torture.[21] There had to be at least "half proof" against the suspect, what American lawyers might call "probable cause," before torture could be administered. These safeguards were designed to assure that only those persons highly likely to be guilty would be examined under torture. Further, torture was supposed to be given, not to achieve a guilty plea, but solely to obtain details that only a guilty person would know and that could be verified, e.g., what weapon did you use, where did you hide it.

Roman law, which had such a dominating impact on canon law, which in turn influenced civil law, was very concerned not only with laying down basic principles of law, but also with so defining terms and procedures that in so far as possible absolute objectivity was maintained, leaving little to the discretion of the judge, who was simply to apply the law. As a result the application of Roman law was universal, permitting little leeway for the judge to soften its hard and fast rules even in the presence of mitigating circumstances. Hence the law was harsh but fair. The Napoleonic Code brought statutory law to a high degree of refinement in this regard.

Torture itself was of Roman origin. Roman law in the days of the Republic permitted only a slave or a provincial to be tortured. However, in the early days of the Empire the custom was begun of subjecting to this process of examination a Roman citizen accused of treason. From then on, references to torture are numerous in the Roman codes, which came to be of general application. It is therefore not suprising that the diffusion of torture coincides with the Reception of Roman Law by the legists of the Bologna school, though some authors claim that the Germans customarily used torture even before the revival of Roman law in Europe. In any case, torture was customarily employed in secular courts in the high Middle Ages and remained as an integral part of criminal proceedings in the common law of Europe down to the French Revolution.

As far as canon law is concerned, torture entered by a different route. Though it was common in Europe it was not envisaged for ecclesiastical trials. By one of the quirks of legal history, which regards the wording of the law as sacrosanct, the process whereby a citizen of Rome accused of treason could be tortured, and, if guilty even be put to death, was taken up by Pope Innocent III for quite a different reason. He stated in his constitution of 1199 *Vergentis in senium* that since in common law persons guilty of the crime of treason were punished by death and the confiscation of their property, so much the more should those who strayed from the Faith and offended God be inflicted with ecclesiastical censure and confiscation of their property, for it was far more serious to injure divine majesty than human. The pope used this analogy to indicate why confiscation of heretics' property was in accordance with common law. He never considered torture or the death penalty for heresy - quite the contrary. And in the final codification of his decrees in regard to heretics in the Fourth Lateran Council, no mention is made either of torture or the death penalty - nor were they employed by the Church.

However, in the convoluted ways whereby legal practice

develops, Pope Innocent IV, also a canon lawyer, used a similar comparison to justify the use of torture and, as we will see, to explain the death penalty decreed by secular rulers. In a decree of 1252 directed to the cities of northern Italy, Innocent IV empowered the podesta or ruler of the city, among other provisions:

> to force all captured heretics, without injury to their persons or danger of death, to confess their errors and denounce other heretics whom they know. For just as thieves and robbers of material things are forced to denounce their accomplices and to confess their crimes, so should heretics who are truly thieves, murderers of souls, and robbers of the sacraments of God and of the Christian Faith.[22]

This permission to secular authorities was intended for northern Italy and seems not to have been utilized in Languedoc during this period. Indeed no firm references to the use of torture by the Inquisition are to be found in surviving documents through the end of the thirteenth century.[23] Other, less drastic means, it appears, were employed to pressure witnesses to reveal what they knew: close imprisonment, chaining in small cells, restrictions on food. Physical torture seems not to have been part of the ordinary scene of the inquisitorial procedure in Languedoc at the height of the Inquisition.

Unfortunately, torture did continue as a legal method for obtaining evidence in secular courts all over Europe throughout the late Middle Ages and well into the High Renaissance, and beyond. England under the Tudors equated heresy with treason, and by order of the Privy Council the Jesuit Edmund Campion, among others, was tortured and eventually hanged, drawn and quartered at Tyburn Hill. The charge? He was a Catholic priest living in England. In time, torture was no longer employed in Europe, not because it came to be perceived as being inhumane (it had always been recognized as being a repulsive way of obtaining evidence), but because circumstantial evidence came to be accepted as sufficient proof to convict. The reasons for this change may be found in the later development of more centralized governments, codified laws, professional judges and lawyers, the omnipresence of trained police, and a variety of punishments other than death for the commissions of felonies, e.g., prisons, the galleys, workhouses, exile, etc. With the emergence of the jury system the legal proofs which were required to be present in order to convict were done away with. Now all that is necessary is that the jury be 'thoroughly convinced.' As professor Langbein comments:

> "The jury standard of proof made it unnecessary to provide extensive and refined evidence-gathering. An English jury could still convict on whatever evidence persuaded it, it could still convict on less evidence than was required as a precondition for investigation under torture on the Continent."[24]

Adhémar Esmein puts the matter of evaluating evidence, "the stiffest crux for the law courts," in even stronger language:

> "What appears to stand out prominently is the feeling that there is here an arbitrary power, to solve the most formidable question which can be propounded to mortal men. The jury appears to be placed above the law and authorized to judge on an *impression*. It is to this formula even more than to the system of the moral proof that the false doctrine of the *omnipotence* of the jury must be traced."[25]

Finally, Tarde speaks to the point:

> "Even the jury was destined to furnish the illusion of certainty. A presumption of oracular infallibility was attached by religious belief, as later on by philosophical

> and humanitarian belief, to decisions, *the grounds of which were not stated.* Furthermore, from its origin, as we see, the verdict has only been, as it is still in our day, a supreme act of opinion, a 'constat' of fact and not a judgement properly speaking ....''[26]

Methods of proof for determining the guilt or innocence of an accused person have a long history in the development of legal procedure. The Middle Ages adopted so-called non-rational appeals to the "judgement of God," ordeals and trial by combat. When this was felt to be unsatisfactory - and in fact was prohibited - another means of proof had to be found in order to satisfy the juridic demands of sufficient proof to justify acquittal or conviction. Forced confession, torture, was employed, because this assured "full proof," a confession of guilt, and hence a legal condemnation. With the emergence of centralized governments, trained judges, public prosecutors, and local police forces torture was no longer needed or permitted. Better means had been found. But what about the twentieth century? What justification can there be for over sixty nations whose governments systematically practice or, at the very least, tolerate the use of torture?

> "In 1874, Victor Hugo could say 'torture has once and for all ceased to exist.' Today we are compelled to recognize that it is more widespread than ever before. In more than a third of the United Nations, torture is used either as a method of interrogation or as a means of punishing detainees. Torture knows no idealogical frontiers: it is practiced in Iran, Iraq, Ethiopia, Uganda, Guinea, South Africa, Guatemala, Argentina, Chile, Bolivia, Nicaragua, Indonesia, Bangladesh, Afghanistan, USSR, Morocco, Tunisia, Israel and the People's Republic of Yemen.''[27]

CHAPTER V
SENTENCES AND PENANCES FOR THOSE CONVICTED

In the course of their investigation of the presence of heresy in the regions designated by their appointment, the Inquisitors interviewed literally thousands of people. The General Summons included all members of a particular parish or of an entire town. The Individual Summons was directed at persons against whom some information had been lodged. It is, then, impossible to estimate the number of people who actually testified before the inquisitorial tribunal. The only figures available pertain to those against whom definite allegations had been entered and who had been tried in the inquisitorial court. Even here the numbers are sketchy because of the incomplete nature of the relevant documents and the total lack of most of the registers which recorded the actual sentences. Nevertheless we do have some records which do state the specific types of penances handed down, the number of persons involved, and the fulfillment, or the avoidance as often occurred, of the sentence.

After the actual trial of the accused had been completed, all the evidence was sifted through by the staff of the tribunal, the assessors, the *jurisperiti*, and the good men (*boni viri*). In light of all this a decision as to guilt or innocence was determined upon by the Inquisitor. Next, the local bishop was given the record, and he and the Inquisitor agreed on an appropriate penance. If they disagreed the case in its entirety was to be referred to the pope. Sentence could only be imposed upon those who agreed to accept it and this promise was made part of the written record.[1] If the guilty did not consent to perform their penance, however, they were thereby declared to be contumacious, and hence to be heretics with the consequent confiscation of their property.[2]

After a number of cases had been tried in a town or a region a general concourse was assembled on a given Sunday to assure the greatest possible effect on the community. The local bishop, the clergy and all the populace gathered to hear a General Sermon. The Inquisitor delivered a discourse covering the main articles of the Faith, stressing those beliefs which had come under attack by the local heretics. All were requested to renounce any heretical doctrines to which they may have given adherence. Then the sentences were read out by the Inquisitor to all those present including the ones receiving the verdicts.

The types of penances that were handed down.

Traditionally, the Church has always taught that she, like the State, is a perfect society. Consequently, she has the right to all the means appropriate to attain her end, the sanctification and salvation of her members. Since the faithful are not only spiritual, but physical as well, the Church makes use of two types of penances in correcting erring members: spiritual and temporal. The spiritual censures are Excommunication, Interdict, and Suspension. The temporal penances in the period with which we are dealing were mainly almsgiving, pious works, visiting churches, pilgrimages to various shrines, mandatory presence at church functions wearing signs of penitence and subject to ritual flagellation, wearing crosses of different colors in public, fines, confiscations, destruction of buildings, imprisonment, and various legal disqualifications consequent upon a declaration of infamy. Penalties are also classified according to whether their purpose is medicinal, that is, the hope that the person will thereby come to see the error of his ways and reform - promoting the principle of atonement rather than punishment; or vindictive, if the intent is to render satisfaction or expiation for the crime. For instance:

> *Excommunication* excludes one from the community of the faithful with the consequent deprivation of the right to assist at Divine Services, or receive the Sacraments and Christian burial.

Interdict prohibits Divine Services, Christian burial, the Sacraments and the sacramentals in a named church or locality.

Suspension prohibits a cleric from exercising his office.

The penances handed down by the Inquisition were usually one or more of the following:

1. *Pilgrimage.*[3] One of the most popular devotions of the Middle Ages was the undertaking of a penitential journey to a famous religious shrine, in atonement for one's sins, to seek the special assistance of the Saint, and to gain the many indulgences granted for such a pious work. These at times difficult journeys were undertaken voluntarily for one's spiritual benefit, even as they are made today—for example, to the Holy Land in Israel, to Saint Peter's in Rome, to the shrine of Our Lady of Lourdes in southern France, although today the trip is rarely made on foot, or in groups wearing simple garb, carrying the pilgrim's staff, and joining in alternate prayer and meditation. Pilgrimages also could be assigned as a penance, and this was often done by the inquisitorial tribunal in the case of heresy. Hence the repentant heretic would make his way over the mountains along the famous "pilgrims' road" to the shrine of Saint James of Compostella in the north western province of Spain, or to Canterbury to the tomb of Saint Thomas, or to the shrine of the three kings at Cologne. Minor pilgrimages were made to a great number of shrines in France itself. The most favored - and the most arduous - was that "overseas", following the crusaders' paths to the Holy Land, and indeed often to join the crusaders themselves. This long and dangerous journey could take years; the sentences at times indicate three to five years. The Emperor Frederick II promised many times to go, was reminded just as many times by the Popes of his unfulfilled vow, and finally went. Indeed he had himself crowned in Jerusalem! At the peace treaty of

Paris in 1229, Count Raymond VII of Toulouse engaged himself to spend five years in Palestine as part of his reconciliation with the Church and the King, but he never got there. Many repentant heretics did fulfill their promises to visit such shrines, had their papers on which the Inquisitor had written their sentence duly notarized by the rector of the assigned shrine, and brought them back as an affidavit of their compliance. In hardship cases, these pilgrimages were often commuted to other, less arduous exercises. Also it was found that sending penitent heretics to the Holy Land was at times counterproductive, for some of these supposed converts spread their heretical doctrines in the Levant.

2. *The wearing of crosses*

One of the lesser public penances was the wearing of yellow cloth crosses on the breast and on the shoulders in public for varying lengths of time. It was a simple penance but one that was particularly odious for obvious reasons. It exposed the wearer to public obloquy and made social relations most unpleasant. Sometimes the wearing of crosses was imposed as a mitigation of a more severe sentence, e.g., instead of imprisonment. Other times it was conjoined with other penances, e.g., pilgrimages, visiting churches, ritual flagellation. At times it was the sole punishment. The local pastor had the responsibility of checking on the fulfillment of the sentence. However, as in other instances, Provincial Councils had to take cognizance of abuse tendered these penitents, and had to threaten offenders with the same punishment if they did not cease and desist. Conversely, if the penitent did not wear the crosses or removed them before the stated time, he was liable to the confiscation of his property.

So much for the law. Indeed in order to preclude, so they thought, any ingenious ameliorations the Inquisitors stated most precisely the specifications: the color must be yellow; that the yellow crosses must be worn over a simple garment, which itself could not be yellow; and they gave the person the yellow cloth to be used. Human ingenuity, however, is not so easily thwarted. Some wore cloaks over the crosses; others moved to another town; many simply ceased wearing them at all. It became a game to see who could think of a new way of reducing its effect.

Ritual flagellation.

As a chastisement for a public offense, ritual flagellation was imposed as a penalty by itself or in conjunction with another penance, e.g., wearing of crosses. The procedure called for the penitent to walk barefoot in the procession through the church, carrying a candle in one hand and a whip in the other. At a given point in the service he surrendered the candle and, giving the whip to the celebrant, knelt to receive the discipline. Raymond VI, Count of Toulouse, underwent ritual flagellation for being a supporter of heresy at the church of Saint-Gilles from the Papal Legate Milo. It will be recalled that King Henry II of England submitted to ritual flagellation in a similar manner at Canterbury Cathedral for his alleged complicity in the martyrdom of Saint Thomas, the archbishop, in that very cathedral. These flagellations usually took place at the Sunday Mass and in the solemn processions on great feast days.

3. *Fines.*

The giving of alms has a long tradition in the Church, and it was early adopted as a form of penance. The Inquisition adopted this mode, too, but early on both the Pope and Provincial Councils cautioned the Dominican Friars against imposing monetary fines because of the inevitable unfavorable insinuations that would be made against their Order and the Church. Pope Innocent IV permitted the levying of fines when no other punishment seemed in order, with the usual reservation that the monies realized be utilized for charitable works or for the expenses of the inquisitorial tribunal. For example, it was felt that a fine was particularly suitable for the avaricious rich, who might find this assessment painfully distasteful. Further it was found that such pledges might well act as surety bonds for those released, to guarantee their fidelity. More often that not, fines were levied to accomplish some good work, e.g., to support a poor person for life, to assist in the expenses of a convent, to rebuild the city walls, to construct a chapel, to furnish an altar, to renovate a cemetery, to donate a window for the local church.

4. *Demolition of houses.*

Strange as it may seem, this is an ancient as well as a contemporary form of retribution. Republican Rome leveled Carthage and plowed it with salt, so that it could not be rebuilt. Today countries bulldoze homes of alleged terrorists. Thus houses of convicted heretics were demolished more as a symbolic penalty to efface the memory of what had happened there. This was particularly true of places where heretics were accustomed to assemble. Further, like Carthage, the homes were not permitted to be rebuilt, but were to be left desolate. However this practice came into conflict with the right of confiscation of the property of heretics - what value was there in a demolished house? In point of fact the destruction of houses was often delayed and in many instances probably never took place at all.[4]

5. *Confiscations.*

One of the most effective means for procuring the cooperation of the feudal nobility in the struggle against heresy was the confiscation of the property of a person who had been convicted of the crime of heresy. In Roman law the crime of heresy was equated with treason, *lèse-majesté,* for which one of the penalties was the confiscation of the property of the offender. In the bull *Vergentis in senium* of 1199, Pope

Innocent III had noted that heresy was far worse then *lèse-majesté,* since it was far more serious to deny divinely revealed truths and thus offend God than it was to denigrate any human ruler. By extension, then, the pope argued that those guilty of heresy should have their property confiscated. Moreover if the civil officials did not render the requisite assistance to church prelates in rooting out heresy they themselves would be subject to the same expropriations. Strictly speaking, the proceeds from such seizures pertained to the Church only in those areas over which it exercised political dominion, the Patrimony of Saint Peter in Italy. Everywhere else all confiscated property belonged by law to the king or emperor, or one who enjoyed regalian rights. For instance, by special arrangements between the French king and the count of Toulouse, the Count was the recipient of all such forfeitures. When Raymond VII died, his successor, Alphonse of Poitiers, (1249-1271), enjoyed the same privilege; after his death, however, it reverted to the crown.

In all this ecclesiastical legislation the Pope was careful to preserve the dominant rights of the suzerain. King Philip II of France was quite unhappy with the Pope's permitting the transfer of feudal fiefs from a heretic to a faithful noble, though he had no quarrel with the principle of confiscation since he himself was by law the beneficiary. It was the intent of the pope that these expropriations be made, not out of cupidity, but for correction, and that the accruals were to be put to pious uses for the public utility. This could remain a pious wish, for seizures were made by secular rulers who decided themselves how the seized properties were to be disposed of. There existed some Church legislation indicating how these properties should be divided - a half here, a quarter there - but except in strictly papal territories, it had no effect in law.

In theory, this system of confiscations would seem to open the door to great profit for the confiscating ruler - and undoubtedly it did in given cases. There were abuses, as the Popes had to protest over and over again to the French king because of premature seizures of properties of heretical suspects who had not yet been tried. But as the needs of the Inquisitorial tribunal became more apparent, particularly in the construction and maintenance of prisons, and the support and feeding of the inmates, which the French King and the Count of Toulouse, Alphonse of Poitiers, undertook to supply in the Midi - who else could do it? - the apparent profits dwindled. Indeed so demanding did the expense of maintaining prisoners become that there is a heavy suspicion that certain officials of the Count of Toulouse took occasion to burn, on their own authority, relapsed heretics who had been imprisoned for life. Fewer mouths to feed![5] This unspeakable conduct was bitterly protested by the Inquisitor. It appears that the great vassals who had the legal duty of providing for the prisons from their expropriations took this incumbrance but lightly. The king alone and Alphonse of Poitiers regularly contributed to the expenses of the inquisitorial offices and prisons.

6. *Imprisonment.*

One of the anomalies of the Middle Ages was that there were practically no prisons for the containment of those convicted of serious crimes. What prisons there were had for their purpose the retention of prisoners prior, merely, to their trials. The great legal historian Frederick W. Maitland has noted the reason for this situation, succinctly:

> The one punishment that can easily be inflicted by a state which has no apparatus of prisons and penitentiaries is death.[6]

Death and mutilation were the accepted punishments for convicted felons in the legal codes of the Middle Ages.

Against this peremptory, harsh code, the Church put forth its traditional abhorrence of bloodshed and exercised its influence to turn secular legislation away from blood sanctions. She introduced the idea of atonement, that the sinner, given time, would turn from his evil ways and amend his life - and cautioned that this time of grace should not be abruptly cut short by an immediate death sentence. There was a long list of felonies for which the only punishment was death or mutilation. However under the impetus of the Church other means found their way into secular legislation.

Impelled then to evolve a more humane method for dealing with serious delinquencies, the Church recommended imprisonment, whereby the convicted heretic might have time to meditate on his errors and might hopefully return to the Catholic Faith. At the same time she protected the faithful from being corrupted by heretical doctrine. Hence, the Church considered imprisonment a medicinal penalty, not a vindictive one. This change in punishing a major crime necessitated the construction of prisons. For while some of the religious buildings could be adapted for this purpose, their number was limited. Construction of prisons, however, required money and materials, both in short supply. The first ones were built at Toulouse and at Carcassonne, for the latter of which the king paid. Another prison was prepared at the beginning of the fourteenth century by Jacques Fournier, Bishop of Pamiers, who later became Pope Benedict XII, and whose inquisitorial registers have survived.[7] The prisons were referred to as "the wall" from the Latin *murus,* the cell in which the prisoner was confined in strict isolation. The "large wall" was a much larger room with many inmates. In spite of repeated injunctions, single cells simply could not be provided for everyone. The church edifices were not built in that fashion, and hence most of the prisoners lived in common halls and were comparatively free to move about. Providing sustenance was a problem and an expense, so that the plainness of food was almost guaranteed. The king's only instruction to his seneschal at the

Carcassonne prison was to see to it that they received bread and water daily. Strict incarceration was quite another matter. These individual cells were usually in the cellar, and the inmate was in irons. Fortunately, it appears that very few were sentenced to such strict confinement. Upon hearing complaints about these conditions Pope Clement V (1305-1314) sent a commission of Cardinals to investigate. The conditions they found were lamentable: lack of beds, meagre nourishment, and chains. It is also true, it appears, that escape even from these cells was not infrequent, particularly at night, since the surveillance was something less than all-pervasive.

7. *The death penalty.*

From the days of Charlemagne (800-814), Christendom meant the unity of Faith and political loyalty throughout Europe. All citizens of whatever political allegiance firmly believed that any deviation from the common Faith posed a threat to the unity and stability of the political and social fabric. Hence both Church and State had their own legislation regarding heresy. Multiple prescriptions of the Roman Code attest to a like attitude on the part of the Roman Empire at an earlier date, such crimes being regarded as most serious. The Church as spiritual vicar acted first. The Inquisitor tried to explain the true doctrine and to correct erring members. If, however, an individual refused after having relapsed to repent, the church, recognizing its failure, declared him a heretic, withdrew its support and "abandoned" him to the secular authority, which proceeded to apply its own law. The fact that this procedure was not always followed - that enraged mobs seized suspects and summarily burned them - demonstrates the popular feeling towards such crimes and also the tenuous nature of the feudal governments of that age.

Such was the milieu within which one must view the ultimate penalty which society then exacted for what Romans before them and the Tudors afterwards termed treason. As for the Church, the various penances given to heretics and their adherents have been enumerated: pilgrimages, wearing yellow crosses, ritual flagellation, fines, confiscation, destruction of houses, and imprisonment - all of which were meant to be medicinal, intended to give the heretic time to repent and return to the true Faith. But the secular authority had other laws, including the death penalty, which seems to have been the only punishment envisaged for capital crimes, with the possible exception of mutilation. A rough age, but so it was. "The worst cruelties," Maitland, however, states, "belong to a politer time."[8] Renaissance Germany's code hardly erred on the side of softness. Captial punishments there included hanging in chains, beheading, burning to death, stoning, throwing from a cliff to the rocks below, drowning, the smashing of limbs and tying to a wheel to die in agony. Treason was thought to merit being hanged, drawn and quartered - a refinement favored by the English Tudors. Less serious crimes drew flogging; loss of ears, nose, upper lip, hands and feet; cutting out of the tongue, and castration. Imprisonment was not favored.[9]

At the height of the Roman Empire the legal code prescribed death for the Manichean heretics, dualists who taught the existence of a good god and a bad god (later these Manicheans were thought to be the progenitors of the medieval Cathars). During the early Middle Ages only the church dealt with heresy, and her sanctions were the usual canonical ones. With the Reception of Roman Law and through the eleventh, twelfth and early thirteenth centuries a change occurred in the attitude of the various peoples toward dissident elements in their midst. In northern France and in Germany beyond the Rhine, heretics were in this period generally pursued and burned without benefit of any law or positive custom, while in southern France and Italy the usual penalty was confiscation and exile.

With the commencement of the thirteenth century the crime of heresy was considered a felony properly so-called, both in the north and in the Midi, and was punishable under the laws and customs. Peter II of Aragon threatened heretics with the stake if they were seized after 1198. King Louis VIII in 1226 and Louis IX in 1228 decreed serious penalties for those condemned as heretics by the church. The current customary law echoed the same theme, in this case, death. All through this period German custom preferred the stake. Although this was not true of imperial holdings in Italy, Frederick II changed it for Lombardy in 1224, decreeing the stake or the cutting out of tongues for heretics. But this ukase seems not to have been enforced. It was not until 1238/39 that Frederick II issued imperial constitutions decreeing the stake for heretics in all parts of his empire, including Provence, and saw to it that these laws were in fact put into effect. And it was not until some years later that these imperial constitutions *in toto* found their way into the official papal registers. The pope thereby acknowledged the secular laws then in force.

Only obdurate heretics and those who had once recanted and then afterwards returned to their former heresy were abandoned to the secular authority, for in the latter case it was deemed that the first conversion had been feigned. This action signified that all the paternal instructions to the accused had failed and the church could do no more. Now it was time for the secular authority to exercise its jurisdiction and enforce its own laws: for the accused was now declared a heretic, that was how he wanted to be regarded. All of these prescriptions, however, permitted the Inquisitor some leeway in applying them and on occasion he could mitigate the sentence of a relapsed heretic to life imprisonment. So it was, for instance, in the case of the Inquisitor Bernard of Caux, who often reduced the sentence to prison instead of releasing the heretic to the political power.

During this period, the middle and late thirteenth century, the legal punishment for heretics was death at the stake, apparently a symbolic act to purge the world of the stain of heresy. It had been employed by irate mobs from time to time without benefit of any judicial condemnation. The Romans had earlier applied the flames for a number of crimes (e.g. the burning of many Christians by the Emperor Galerius.) Finally, the already mentioned laws of Frederick II as well as the customary law of the middle of the thirteenth century made the stake the ordinary punishment for heretics. William of Pelhisson, a contemporary chronicler, mentions a number of burnings in the area of Toulouse. In the inquisitorial courts themselves the number of condemned heretics surrendered to the secular arm was rather small in comparison with the number of people convicted of heretical activity. Of the 930 sentences of Bernard Gui in the following century only forty-two were abandoned to the state. By a strange quirk, Raymond VII, Count of Toulouse, shortly before he died in 1249, suddenly burned eighty heretics on his own authority![10]

8. *The actual sentences themselves of the inquisitorial tribunal.*

The legends of the brutality of the Inquisition in regard to the numbers of persons sentenced to prison and of those abandoned to the secular power and, consequently burned at the stake, have been embellished through the years. These stories yield but grudgingly to the facts. One author, Louis Halphen, states that in two years, 1246-1248, 192 cases were adjudged at Toulouse, and one counts 192 sentences of imprisonment.[11] Another historian, L. Tanon, asserts that for the same period the Inquisitor Bernard of Caux imposed the penalty of perpetual imprisonment with great abandon and rigor; indeed he says that life imprisonment was the most frequent penalty inflicted.[12]

The extant documents for the period in question do not sustain these assertions. The pertinent documents are hard to come by, and even the ones that have survived must be evaluated according to their juridic validity. Condemnations properly so-called (abandonment to the secular arm, contumacy, posthumous sentences, and sentences to prison) must be contained in an official document authenticated by the actual seals of the Inquisitors and their assessors. This data, then, is absolutely certain. Any documents not having the legal form of a register can only be regarded as an *aide-memoire*, a summary of the actions of the inquisitorial tribunal made by the notaries. These have no legal standing. For lesser penances there exist official documents, the *acta inquisitionis,* which record the written sentence given to each individual together with a separate letter signed by the Inquisitor which the penitent must carry with him. For example, if one was sent on a pilgrimage to the shrine of Saint James of Compostella in Galicia in Spain, he would be given a letter stating this, which he in turn would have attested at Compostella and remit to the Inquisitor on his return as an affidavit of his compliance. Further, from the record of confiscations, since they pertained to the transfer of property and had a long history of legal wrangling in the civil courts, additional information can be gleaned regarding the number condemned as heretics.

Working very carefully from extant registers and other available documents, Professor Yves Dossat estimates that for the years 1245-1246 in the diocese of Toulouse the following figures would seem to be justified.[13] It is estimated that over 5,000 people were interviewed during this period. Out of a total of 945 people who were adjudged guilty in some degree of heretical involvement, some 105 persons were sentenced to prison, while 840 received lesser penances, e.g., wearing of crosses, pilgrimages, etc. There is no way of knowing how many, if any, were abandoned to the secular authority. The above is an extrapolated figure and could very well be close to the truth. Hence one may safely conclude from an analysis of the surviving records that the Inquisitor Bernard of Caux was far less severe than the aforementioned historians have painted him. Only one out of every nine persons who were convicted in this tribunal received a prison sentence, while the most frequent, the ordinary, penance imposed by him was the wearing of crosses. As noted above, a person could not be sentenced unless he agreed to submit to the penalty and this promise was so recorded in the registers. However, it appears that twenty-five percent of those recorded as sentenced to prison for one reason or another did not show up. Of course they would then be declared contumacious, but it does point up the very large discrepancy between recorded sentences and the actual numbers, for instance, who performed their sentences.[14]

After the departure of the Inquisitor Bernard of Caux from Toulouse the data for the tribunal in Toulouse is a little more difficult to interpret; for the records available only note the more serious penances, and none of the lesser ones, for the years 1249 to 1257. Of the 306 major penances for this period, twenty-one were abandoned to the secular arm, 239 received prison terms, thirty fled, eleven deceased were declared to have been heretics, and five relapsed again into heresy. After a painstaking analysis of all available data Professor Dossat concludes that for the middle of the thirteenth century only one out of every hundred heretics sentenced by the Inquisition was abandoned to the secular power, while between ten and twelve percent received prison sentences. Further, the Inquisitors reduced sentences to lesser penances and commuted others. Indeed on occasion they reduced the sentences of even the relapsed heretics to the wearing of crosses. It becomes quite obvious, then, that the number thought to have been sent to the stake must be considerably reduced. And many of those burned had been condemned posthumously.[15]

Appeals from the verdicts of the Inquisitors to Rome.

One of the passionate criticisms of the twentieth century legalists is that "in these inquisitorial trials resulting in either loss of life or immuration and confiscation of property, there was no appeal from the court."[16] In the Roman Republic, it is true, there was no appeal in the sense of invoking the aid of a superior judge for the purpose of obtaining redress against an injury or grievance, either already inflicted or about to be inflicted by an inferior judge. How could one question the decisions of one's peers? Such an idea was repugnant to the conception of judicial infallibility of popular judges. Moreover it presumed the existence of a hierarchy of tribunals. It was not until the Roman Empire perfected its superb code of laws that appeals made their appearance. The Church adopted these prescriptions of the Justinian Code and applied them to ecclesiastical processes. But throughout the early and high Middle Ages "this method of recourse was unknown either to the Germanic or the feudal procedures, both essentially based on popular customs."[17] It was unthinkable to challenge "the judgment of God," the ordeals, or popular justice. It was the Church that preserved and implemented the right of recourse to a higher judge throughout the Middle Ages. Eventually with the organization of the national states in Europe secular courts began to introduce appeals under the influence of Roman and Canon Law.

Although Justinian abolished appeals from decisions made by a judge during the course of a trial - interlocutory decrees - the Church permitted appeals against both interlocutory and final sentences in spite of the abuses that inevitably crept in. The right of appeal was denied to no one, even excommunicates and convicted heretics. The only reservation entered against the right to appeal was any attempt to deliberately frustrate the work of the court or in cases where the law specifically removed this privilege, "*appelatione remota.*" In the Decretals of Gregory IX, appeals were declared to be a remedy for the unjustly oppressed and a legitimate defense of innocence, and they were not to be used or tolerated as a protection of iniquity. Appeals were termed "frivolous" when based on futile or inane reasons, "frustratory" when made merely for the purpose of delaying the just execution of the sentence or of prolonging the final settlement of the trial itself. This mode of defense was adopted by the Church in order to preclude in so far as possible injustice arising from the error, ignorance or prejudice of judges or of the litigant.

Well into the thirteenth century, litigants in church courts were guaranteed all the traditional methods of defense, including the right of appeal. Heresy trials were no exception to this rule. Pope Innocent III heard a number of appeals in such cases and usually committed the re-hearing to his legate on the spot, or called the case to Rome, very often adding the phrase *"appelatione remota."* However, as the Roman Emperors had found before him, there was never a lack of unscrupulous persons who utilized the right of appeal to hinder rather than to obtain justice and thus hamstring the operation of the courts themselves. Thus it was that frivolous and frustratory appeals were denied, while the phrase "*appellatione remota*" under Innocent III applied in full force only against relapsed heretics.

As we have already seen, the same reasons that impelled Pope Gregory IX to institute the inquisitorial tribunal as a court of exception, after some years of experience also led the popes to withdraw certain refinements of the judicial processes because of the nature of the crime of heresy and its widespread growth. The right of appeal was one such restriction, but as in similar matters practice differed considerably from theory. While the phrase *"appelatione remota"* appeared increasingly in papal documents, Gregory IX continued the tradition of handling each appeal on its merits. The relevant documents reveal that this pope was particularly sensitive to such appeals and repeatedly requested re-investigations in order to determine the truth of cases reaching him, including appeals from relapsed heretics.[18]

His successor, Pope Innocent IV, maintained a very tight grip on the operations of the inquisitorial tribunals. Despite the use of the limiting phrase, *"appelatione remota,"* the pope repeatedly entertained appeals made to him by complainants and voided unjust decisions. Indeed so often did Innocent revise the sentences of the Inquisitors that the Dominicans and a number of the local bishops felt that the whole process of the court was imperiled. In fact he suspended the operation of the Inquisition for a time and the Dominican Inquisitors simply withdrew in frustration. This serious impasse was not finally resolved until after the death of Innocent.[19]

It appears, then, that throughout this whole period appeals found their way to Rome for redress. Although heresy was considered a present, imminent danger demanding immediate disciplinary action and admitting of no delay, nevertheless appeals were heard. In these circumstances a court of exception, such as was the Inquisition, enjoyed unquestioned competency and exercised the right of deciding cases. But the pope, in spite of the apparent prohibition of appeals, *"appelatione remota,"* continued to oversee the operations of the Inquisition and remedied injustices wherever he found them.

Modeled on the long forgotten regulations of the Code of Justinian, the Church brought a new procedure into the legislation of the Middle Ages. Appeals were quite out of character for the local, feudal, manorial courts. "Secular justice, administered chiefly by hundreds of petty independent barons and princes, was local and weak, selfish and mercenary, crude and unprogressive," in the words of John Wigmore,[20] a legal historian. The ever present right of appeal to Rome in ecclesiastical courts exercised a salutary affect on inquisitorial tribunals and enabled the pontiff to satisfy himself that inequities were remedied and unworthy judges removed and false rumors dissipated. The success of the church system of justice was not lost on secular rulers, who eventually adopted appeals as a regular procedure in their reorganized and centralized court systems.[21]

CHAPTER VI
EPILOGUE

For us in the twentieth century it is most difficult to appreciate the intellectual ferment and the flourishing culture that so characterized the brilliant thirteenth century. It was the age of the scintillating universities of Paris, Toulouse, Montpellier, Oxford, Cambridge, Salerno, Bologna, Salamanca; of scholastic philosophy and Thomas Aquinas, Bonaventure, and Roger Bacon; of epics and romances: the *Nibelungenlied,* the *Cid,* Arthur's Knights of the Round Table, the *Romance of the Rose,* the trouvères and the troubadours in Provence, and Dante's *Divine Comedy.* It witnessed the flowering of a luminous spiritual growth: St. Francis of Assisi, O.F.M. (1181-1226) and St. Clare of the Second Order Franciscans (1193-1253); the theological giants but first saints: St. Thomas Aquinas, O.P. (1225-1274), St. Albert the Great, O.P. (1206-1280), St. Bonaventure, O.F.M. (1221-1274); St. Louis IX, King of France (1214-1297) and St. Margaret, a peasant of Cortona, Italy (1247-1297); St. Dominic, O.P. (1170-1221) and St. Nicholas of Tolentine, O.S.A. (1245-1305); St. Clare of Montefalco, O.S.A. (1268-1308); St. Antony of Padua of Portugal (1195-1231) and St. Raymond of Pennafort, O.P. from Spain (1175-1275). The heavy Romanesque architecture had seen itself surpassed by the soaring Gothic Cathedrals of Chartres, St. Denis, Notre Dame, and Bourges whose stained glass windows have never been equaled. Bishops and kings, knights and peasants forever render homage to the heavenly court in the glorious rosettes and multi-colored windows of Sainte Chapelle and Chartres. The sonorous Gregorian Chant resounded from a thousand-choir stalls with the solemn *Dies Irae* and the triumphant *Te Deum.*

The world has rolled on to the Renaissance, the Protestant Reformation, the Enlightenment, the French Revolution, the Age of Realism and the Commercial Revolution, down to our own day of high technology and nuclear power, instant communication and all pervasive centralized administration — and sensitiveness to human rights.

It is only with a sustained effort that one can re-create the *Weltanschauung* of the Middle Ages at its height. Particularly is it demanding to realize that a previous culture quite as lustrous as our own viewed religion as an integral part of their civilization; that the thirteenth century represented only a milestone in the continuing evolution of institutions and law, neither retrogressing on the one hand, nor anticipating on the other the improvements achieved by later centuries.

For the citizen of medieval Europe belief in and the practice of the Roman Catholic religion was regarded as essential to the maintenance and stability of the social fabric. Today there is a multiplicity of religious creeds and even an outright disbelief in even the existence of a personal God; secularism is the order of the day.

To preach that marriage was evil, that all oaths were forbidden, that religious suicide (*endura*) was good, that man had no free will and therefore could not be held responsibile for his actions, that civil authority had no right either to punish criminals or to defend the country militarily, seemed in the view of the medieval man to strike at the very root of society. Today many of these principles have been challenged.

In a departure from the traditional attitude of Roman Law and feudal custom the inquisitorial procedure of the thirteenth century determined that crime should no longer be viewed as a personal offense between two private individuals but rather as a public felony inimical to the peace and tranquillity of the commonweal; that evidence should be weighed and judged in court; that a trained judge should pass on the principles of law and fact as presented by a public prosecutor in the name of the community; that appeals from the decisions and sentences of the court should be permitted; that punishments other than death or mutilation should be utilized, e.g., imprisonment. All of these innovations were subsequently adopted by all the civil courts of Europe, and we take them for granted today — however we may honor them in the breach, e.g., continuing data from Amnesty International.

Restrictions on the right to cross-examine witnesses, and on the presence of defense attorneys because of the tenuous social and political conditions then current, as well as the use of torture because of the lack of better legal methods: all of these appear to modern readers as particularly odious.

As in the days of antiquity and throughout the Roman Empire, heresy was regarded as a political and social as well as a religious crime in the unitary society of medieval Christendom. In the Inquisition, when the Inquisitor was unable to convince the accused of the error of his ways, the declared heretic was "abandoned" to the secular ruler, who now proceeded to enforce the civil penalty for the crime: confiscation and death — they had no other. Today religion, for many, is personal to the individual, and irrelevant to society.

In all of this it would seem to be axiomatic that a person should be inviolable in his mind and body, however much pressing historical circumstances might seem to justify violating the one or the other. Indeed Pope Pius XII in his allocution to the officials of the Rota (October 6, 1946) said:

> Undoubtedly in the course of the centuries, the tribunal for the defense of the Faith [i.e., the Inquisition] may have assumed forms and methods which were not demanded by the nature of things, but which find their explanation in the light of the particular historical circumstances.... If the modern conscience feels that the measures taken in past centuries against attacks on the Faith overstepped the limits of justice, in its turn our modern society generally shows an unwarrantable insensitiveness and indifference to this matter.

Finally, in the "Declaration on Religious Liberty," Vatican Council II on December 7, 1965 stated:

> Although in the life of the people of God in its pilgrimage through the vicissitudes of human history

there has at times appeared a form of behavior which was hardly in keeping with the spirit of the Gospel and was even opposed to it, it has always remained the teaching of the Church that no one is to be coerced into believing. Thus the leaven of the Gospel has long been at work in the minds of men and has contributed greatly to a wider recognition by them in the course of time of their dignity as persons. It has contributed too to the growth of the conviction that in religious matters the human person should be kept free from all manner of coercion in civil society.

APPENDIX I
HISTORIOGRAPHY OF CATHARISM

Henri Maisonneuve, *Historiographie du Catharisme* (Cahiers de Fanjeaux, XIV). Toulouse, Privat, 1979. in-8, 443, *Revue d'histoire ecclésiastique* (Compte Rendu). Vol. LXXVI, No. 2 (April–June, 1981) 386–391.

This fourteenth volume "does not purport to compose a history of Catharism, but a history of this history," writes Father Vicaire in the Introduction. It appears scarcely possible, indeed, to write here and now an exhaustive history of Catharism, despite the noteworthy works of these last years, but it is not without interest to know what the writers who, from the thirteenth to the twentieth century, studied the "Cathar phenomenon," have thought about it. This is what these fifteen contributions of the Cahier tell us.

From the Albigensian Crusade to the Wars of Religion, Catharism is chiefly known from works of its adversaries and the documents of the Inquisition. But from the second half of the sixteenth century, it interests Catholics and Protestants, not as an object of research, but as a subject of polemics. Father M. H. Vicaire, "The Albigensian ancestors of the Protestants: Catholic Comparisons," (23–46), presents some examples of this literature. Our authors establish a ready parallel between Protestants and Cathars; they use against them the argument of prescription which Tertullian used against the heretics of his time; they urge Catherine de Medici and Charles IX to follow the example of Blanche of Castille and St. Louis who put an end to the Albigensian war. The Protestant polemicists, on the contrary, present themselves as authentic witnesses of tradition—G. Bedouelle, "The Albigensians, witnesses of the true gospel: Protestant historiography of the 16th and of the beginning of the 17th century" (47–70), cites many authors who oppose to the argument of prescription that of antiquity: Protestants and Cathars are connected with the primitive Church, that of the just who did not recognize the transformations that men have made the Roman Church undergo. The synods of Languedoc support the same arguments: that of Montauban in 1595 declares: "our religion is ancient and catholic and that of papism is new and private" (57).

Heated polemics are followed by a time of scientific inquiry in a more serene climate: a better knowledge of the contemporary authors of the Albigensian war and of the archives shows to what extent the medieval heresies, notably Catharism, took root in Pyrenean Midi. Local history is not able to ignore them. But to what extent does it know them? Ph. Wolff, "Is there a perspective proper to regional histories, 16th–18th centuries?" (71–84), gives a nuanced response. Of the twelve historians mentioned only two or three have been able to distinguish the different sects, to describe them, to locate them with reference to one another. The most remarkable historian of this period is the Maurist Dom Vaissète: his *Histoire générale du Languedoc* with its notes and supporting documents, appeared from 1730 (completed and re-edited by A. Molinier in 1873 and the years following) is always authoritative. Dom Vaissète not only distinguishes the Cathars from the Waldensians, he searches further from whence they came. With some of the preceding historians, he thinks that the Languedocian Catharism came from the Orient, more precisely from Armenia, via Bulgaria and Italy.

Catharism does not only command the attention of the historians of the country of Old Provençal. R. Darricau, "From a theologian's history to the scientific discipline: Bossuet, 16–18th centuries" (85–117), mentions in some pages the names of scholars and their publications who broaden the field of historical knowledge and at the same time that of theology. In contact with these scholars and their texts, Bossuet acquires a considerable amount of information, which sifted through his critique, furnishes him with the material for his *History of the Variations of the Protestant Churches,* published in 1688. On the way, he encounters medieval heresies, principally Catharism and Waldensianism which he distinguishes perfectly one from the other and of which he presents a description which later expositions will be able to correct, but not destroy. "The most reliable authors of the 18th and 19th centuries," concludes R. Darricau, "ought only to improve his conclusions, in expressing them with greater precision and complementing them with the aid of additional documents" (108).

In what measure are these scholarly conclusions carried over into teaching? H. Duranton, "The Albigensians in the general histories and in the school manuals from the 16th to the 18th centuries'' (119–139), responds in the negative. One reverts to the time of the polemicists. The manuals stress the military operations; Cathar dissidence provokes the crusade, the crusade reaches completion with the triumph of the king, order is re-established; but they do not say in what this dissidence consisted, or else they say so briefly or poorly. However, towards the end of the eighteenth century, the positions are less certain: the monarchial order is contested, the Cathars, victims of intolerance, inspire some pity. But this is without any bearing on a greater knowledge of their doctrine. It is much the same during the greatest part of the 19th century. According to Ch. Olivier Carbonell, ''From Augustine Thierry to Napoleon Peyrat: a half a century of obscurantism, 1820–1870'' (143–162), the political context of the first half of the century saw the resurgence of the old clichés. As the peoples were oppressed by the Holy Alliance of the conservative powers, so were the Cathars, new counterparts to the Protestants in their common opposition to the established powers. This theme, let us call it traditional, presents itself under many aspects: one is anti-clerical; it denounces *à satiété* the corruption of the clergy of the Midi, the fanaticism of the officials of the Church and their cruelty towards the unfortunate Albigensians; the other ignores the religious character of the Albigensian problem; it sees in the crusade only the annihilation of the Provençal culture by the barbarians of the north. Let us not forget that we are in the romantic period where one evokes with emotion the poetry of the landscape, the seignorial retreats and the mysterious chateaus, like Montségur, ''the holy gate, the house of the pure, the abode of the Perfected, the sanctuary of the Gospel and of the romantic Fatherland,'' writes Napoleon Peyrat, anticlerical pastor, romantic and Provençal poet, in his *History of the Albigensians* (1870, 1872). But what does one know of Catharism? The contributions of the two preceding centuries seem completely forgotten. Fortunately, such is not the case.

Everything changes, in effect, with the author of *The History of the Sect of the Cathars or Albigensians,* Paris, 1849, justly called by Yves Dossat, ''The Pioneer: Charles Schmidt'' (163–184). Yves Dossat, after having presented the *curriculum vitae* of Schmidt, an Alsatian Protestant, and the profundity of his research—he has consulted notably the Greek-Slavic sources of Catharism—renders homage to his method and to the soundness of his conclusions. Without doubt, Schmidt has not been able to consult all the sources—he is unaware among other things of *The Treatise against the Bogomiles of Cosmas the Priest* which only appeared in the translation of H. C. Puech and A. Vaillant in 1945—but he confirms now and henceforth the oriental origin of Catharism and its semi-pagan character, "less a Christian heresy than a different religion" (181). We are far from an assimilation to any religious dissident sect, especially to Protestantism.

The objectivity of Schmidt is exceptional. In an another article Ch. Olivier Carbonell, "The liberal Protestant historians or the illusions of a scientific history, 1870–1914," (185–203), denounces the bias of the Protestant historians who reigned in the Sorbonne before the First World War. Under the apparent serenity of the studies on Catharism, published notably in the *Revue historique,* founded in 1876, the anticlerical polemic revives in the official laicism which characterizes the politics in the last years of the nineteenth century. Catharism has no more consistency or value than Catholicism; the two religious organizations who fought each other in the Albigeois are equally obnoxious. Both are dismissed. Of Catharism there is retained, notwithstanding the religious plumage with which it adorns itself—and which the author does not succeed in apprehending—only the anticipatory expression of Protestantism. Three principal names stand out: A. Réville who makes a minute critique of N. Peyrat; Charles Molinier who refuses, *à propos* his thesis in *The Inquisition in the Midi of France in the 13th and 14th centuries,* to study the teachings of the Albigensians; H. Ch. Lea, author of *The History of the Inquisition in the Middle Ages,* published in the United States in 1887, translated into French by S. Reinach in 1900, who describes more readily the vices of the clergy than the teachings of the Cathars.

Faced with the anticlerical attack of the liberal Protestant historians, the Catholic counter-offensive asserted itself with a certain éclat. P. Amargier and A. Ramière de Fortanier, "The Catholic Contribution to the History of Albigensianism, 1866–1916" (205–226) presents the team of the *Revue des questions historiques,* founded in 1866, animated by a conservative spirit, nevertheless sufficiently cognizant of the problems of research and criticism so that it does not lapse into apologetics. From 1885, several names command attention: the future Msgr. Douais whose studies on the Albigensians, the Crusade, the Inquisition are still useful; his best disciple, Msgr. Vidal, who studies notably the Inquisition in the region of Toulouse; particularly Jean Guiraud, professor at the University of Besançon, in 1908 made director of the *Revue des questions historiques,* well-known author of the *History of the Inquisition in the Middle Ages* (1935) and of numerous articles, among others that in which he analyzes the Cathar *consolamentum* according to the Cathar Ritual in the Provençal language published by Clédat in 1887. From it he draws this conclusion that the *consolamentum* is a very old Christian rite of the primitive Church, which projects an entirely new light on the origin of Catharism: "Catharism would appear to us as a primitive Christianity perverted more or less down to the absolute dualism of the Persian Mazdaism and Egyptian metempsychosis by some influences deriving from oriental philosophies and religions" (218).

The "Cathar phenomenon," denuded of all religious content, does not present itself only, as the liberal Protestants think of it, under the aspect of a protest against the vices of the Catholic Church; it would be perhaps even susceptible to a Marxist interpretation, under the aspect of the battle of the classes, an aspect underlined by R. Manselli, "The materialist approaches of the history of Catharism," (229–248). If this question does not pose itself for Marx, it concerns Engels, the German Kautsky, especially the Italian Labriola. The latter sees the heretics of the Middle Ages, not only the Cathars, as so many rebels against the oppression of a clerical society. The fact would be particularly significant in Italy where G. Volpe notes the union of the heretics and the Ghibellines, equally allergic to papal domination. All this is ingenious and perhaps valuable in a certain measure for Italy, but clearly inadequate because the spiritual content of Catharism, as of the other heterodox movements, is eliminated. The question just the same is worth a closer look. Fr. Sanjek, "The dualist phenomenon as seen by the Balkan historians" (249–270), refers to the Bulgarian historians who have analyzed the movement descended from the priest Jeremiah, called

Bogomil, about the tenth century. This Bogomilism is said to be a form of reaction against the temporal power, in this case Hungary, and the spiritual power, the Roman Church. Bogomilism would then be said to be in its origins a social protest movement, opposed to feudalism and to orthodoxy. In Thrace and in Bulgaria, it is tinged, in contact with Paulicianism, with Manichean ideas. However that may be, Bogomilism is supposed to have reached Roumania, indeed Kievan Russia, Bosnia where they may perhaps have created a dissident Church, from where it probably passed into the Occident, not without however undergoing numerous changes in the course of its journeys. Thus, Catharism, heir of Bogomilism, would present an analogous character. It remains nevertheless a mysterious phenomenon.

This mystery even glorifies it with a certain charm, in the magical sense of the term, of which L. Biget, "Mythography of Catharism, 1870–1960" (271–342), analyzes the components: the image of a refined civilization, brutally handled by the Crusade, annihilated by the Inquisition, a theme harped on, but seductive when it adorns itself with the magic of the Romantic style (N. Peyrat); the idealization of victims of intolerance and of obscurantism; the esoteric brilliance come from the Orient, even from the Occident: the legend of the Grail, the treasure of Montségur, the initiation by secret rites into the supreme Knowledge. Under this aspect, there would be a certain analogy, as a matter of fact, however faint, between Catharism and the mystique of superman, symbolized by Nazism, then, after the downfall of Nazism, between Catharism and liberation! This mystery of the legend makes also of Catharism an object of publicity.

In a third article, Ch. Olivier Carbonell, "Vulgarization and regeneration: Catharism through the mass-media" (361–380), denounces the mythical concept of Catharism derived from television; the press, sports and gastronomy: 'rallye et fromages de Montségur'! Catharism, even stripped of its legend, was scarcely known down to our day except by indirect sources permitting its characterization without passion. We have already met on this subject the names of Bossuet, Schmidt, Guiraud. We must now however add some others. In a second contribution, Yves Dossat, "The Discovery of the Cathar texts:

P. Antoine Dondaine, O.P.'' (343–359), recounts in what circumstances Father Dondaine, O.P. ''has opened a new era in the history of Catharism.'' The point here is the discovery of a Florentine manuscript *The Book of the Two Principles,* composed in the second half of the thirteenth century by an Italian Cathar bishop, of a *Compendium for the Instruction of Beginners* and of a Latin ritual, edited by Father Dondaine in 1939, re-edited in the ''Sources chrétiennes'' by Ch. Thouzellier in 1973. There have also been edited a few works of Catholic origin, up to now little or poorly known, which illuminate the history of the Cathar churches of Italy.

Thanks to these discoveries, and not neglecting earlier contributions, is it at last possible to define Catharism other than by what it was not? In a second article, Father M. H. Vicaire, ''Catharism: a religion, 1935–1976'' (381–409), takes stock of the situation. It is certain that the Cathar rites resemble certain rites of Christian antiquity, but their sense is different. The dualist doctrine certainly derives from Bulgarian Bogomilism, perhaps also from Anatolian Paulicianism. But why has this dualist doctrine attracted the people of Languedoc? In truth, what captivates the populace is without doubt less the Manichean idea than the certitude of salvation obtained by the *consolamentum.* ''In its essential inspiration and attitude,'' writes Father Vicaire, ''Catharism . . . is a religion of salvation, a spirituality passionately directed to the certification of a happy death of the *consolamentum* given by the Perfected'' (403). Catharism, although influenced by Oriental heterodoxies, would take its place, finally, like Waldensianism and the other current heretics, in the movement of the spiritual revival of the Middle Ages. But the problem which it poses contains still some particulars which remain without solution.

APPENDIX II
HENRY CHARLES LEA

On the face of it, to take the time and space to indite a critique of H. C. Lea, who wrote almost a century ago, would seem churlish, almost like carrying coals to Newcastle, or erecting a straw man. But, unfortunately, such is not the case. As Professor Henri Maisonneuve has so brilliantly pointed out in his review of *Historiographie du Catharisme* it is the approach, the attitude of the historians rather than scholarly research that has influenced historical writing down through the centuries and the public's reaction towards the Medieval Inquisition—it is not the facts that matter but what people think about it that carries the day.

Even at this late date Lea's books enjoy an all-pervasive influence in the halls of academe not only in the United States but in Europe as well. Unlike the aging of fine wine Lea's works have not improved with the years. What he wrote a century ago remains as written. At the time, Herbert Thurston, S.J., found Lea's writings on Auricular Confession, Indulgences, and the Reformation intolerably biased and inaccurate. G. G. Coulton, Professor of Medieval History at Cambridge University, discovered Father Thurston's critique some 33 years later, and took unmeasured exception to it. Since what Lea and Thurston and Coulton wrote years ago remains current today, it would seem pertinent to continue Henri Maisonneuve's historiographical sketch by looking at two of the most influential writers of this century, Lea and, later, Emmanuel Le Roy Ladurie.

Henry Charles Lea was an American businessman and publisher, son of a Quaker father and a Catholic mother. He was born on September 19, 1825 in Philadelphia, and, his biographer Edward Sculley Bradley tells us: "In 1832, his formal schooling began and ended."[1] His father decided on private tutoring as the best course to follow and his son "remained under the charge of the same tutor, Eugenius Nulty, until he went, at the age of eighteen, to take his place in his father's publishing house. Eugenius Nulty was a unique and interesting character. He had been born in Ireland and bred to the trade of carpenter.

The story is that working one day in a gentleman's library he took down a book and became so interested in it that he began a course of self-prescribed reading and study, and so educated himself."[2]

Thus it happened that Henry Charles Lea never went to school in the ordinary sense of that phrase. In his writings he employed numbers of searchers to go through the archives in Europe and copy manuscripts for him, but he was in no position to make safe generalizations about complicated matters of Church history. Notwithstanding, he published a number of books on the subject:

An historical sketch of celibacy in the Christian church 1867

A history of the Inquisition of the Middle Ages 3 vols. 1887

Chapters from the Religious History of Spain connected with the Inquisition 1890

Formulary of the Papal Penitentiary 1892

History of Auricular Confession and Indulgences 3 vols. 1898

The Moriscos of Spain: their conversion and expulsion 1891

A History of the Inquisition of Spain 4 vols. 1906–07

"The Eve of the Reformation," *Cambridge Modern History* 1902. 2nd edition 1957 eliminated this chapter of Lea.

A History of the Inquisition in the Spanish Dependencies 1908

Early in this century Father Thurston was living in London and writing articles for the journal the MONTH. He was a Jesuit Priest who was educated at St. Malo, France; Mount Saint Mary's (near Sheffield); Stonyhurst College; London University, and was Master of Beaumont College. He joined the staff of the MONTH, in London, and much of his time was spent in the British Museum (now the British Library) searching out documents and books on various topics, mostly pertaining to history, liturgy and hagiography.[3]

In the course of his investigations and research Father Thurston came across a number of Lea's publications which eventually brought forth this remark from him:

"I may say fearlessly," wrote Fr. Thurston, "that it would have been hard to find a writer either more prejudiced or more persistently inaccurate than Dr. H. C. Lea. Had Dr. Lea busied himself with any other subject than the abuses of the Papal system, Lord Acton would have been the very first to denounce him for gross carelessness and want of logic which are conspicuous in almost everything this writer touches."[4]

After reading Lea's chapter "The Eve of the Reformation" in *The Cambridge Modern History* Thurston wrote a critique of it for an American journal in which he concluded:

> A wholly reckless and inaccurate writer like Dr. Lea enjoys a certain immunity from criticism, from the very fact that his misconceptions are so often too fundamental to be investigated in a few minutes or explained in a few lines. The limits of leisure and space preclude the discussion of more than a few choice specimens. But great as may be the industry of Dr. Lea, I believe his capacity for misconception and misrepresentation to be even greater, and the attempts that I have occasionally made to follow up his trail and compare his assertions with his sources, have always ended in a more deeply rooted distrust of every statement made by him. It would be a safe thing probably to say that in any ten consecutive pages ten palpable blunders may be unearthed. At any rate I should like to submit that estimate to the test of experiment. Would Dr. Lea, I wonder, be prepared to accept such a challenge, and to elect to stand or fall by the third volume of his *History of Auricular Confession and Indulgences* or his chapter on the causes of the Reformation in the *Cambridge Modern History?*[5]

At the time, Lea did not respond. Some thirty-three years later G. G. Coulton, Professor of Medieval History at Cambridge University, loudly challenged him to prove his contentions: "I assert with every sense of responsibility that your challenge is libellous and false to a ludicrous and almost inconceivable degree."[6] After numerous other insulting and obnoxious taunts from Coulton,[7] Father Thurston felt constrained to reply. Thus Coulton had his heart's desire, and conditions for a trial by combat were drawn up that would have done credit to Ivanhoe. The works of Lea were given code letters by Coulton, and only these code letters with the number of pages attached were given to Professor G. E. Moore, who wrote down his choice thus: "In complete ignorance of the issue, and therefore with scientific impartiality, I choose ten consecutive numbers at a venture from A 1-522, or B 1-459, or C 1-584, or D 653-691. My choice, as chance directs, is A 200-209."[8] Thurston took Coulton's design in stride and later commented:

> When, therefore, Dr. Coulton, without awaiting my consent, applied to Professor G. E. Moore, who (though he was, to quote his own words, "in complete ignorance of the issue") was good enough to assign at random ten definite pages of Vol. I of the "History of Auricular Confession and Indulgences," I decided to accept the terms proposed. It might, I thought, be good for Dr. Coulton to learn once again[9] the lesson that if his opponents were reluctant to plunge into controversy in answer to his interminable challenges, that reluctance did not necessarily arise from the consciousness that they had nothing to say in reply. I may note that the volume selected was not that which I specially indicated in my American article. Knowing the "Indulgence" volume best, I had proposed Vol. III, but as Vol. I has been settled on, I see no reason to quarrel with the choice made. On the other hand, Dr. Coulton, with a great display of magnanimity, in order that the section might begin and end with a complete paragraph, threw in an extra page and a half. I was free to hunt for errors from the middle of p. 199 to the top of p. 211. But my opponent ends his letter characteristically with these words: "I defy you to find even a single patent blunder in all these twelve pages, and I must put it to you very plainly that you are now in a position which your very worse [sic] policy is that of obstinate muteism [sic]." Did Dr. Coulton, I wonder, intend to write "muleism"?[10]

That was on November 11, 1936. In the *Month* for January and February 1937 there appeared two articles by Thurston, in which were exposed and proved at length some fifteen blunders found in the ten pages chosen by Professor Moore. Father Thurston concluded his two articles thus:

> I submit, then, that by the exposure of the above fifteen blunders Dr. Coulton's challenge has been fairly met. What perhaps impresses me most is the fact that on the surface Dr. Lea presents a case which to the normal reviewer, indolent or otherwise, seems entirely convincing and satisfactory. Even Dr. Coulton, who has given his life to medieval studies, after reading the section selected was so persuaded of its impregnable accuracy that he wrote to me in terms that awaken memories of Bambastes Furioso: "I defy you to find even a single patent blunder in all these twelve pages." The blunders only come to light when, after much toil and waste of time, one investigates the sources appealed to and finds that they say something entirely different from what the American controversialist has read into them. That was my experience thirty-six years ago when I first had occasion to study Dr. Lea's volume on Indulgences. It has been my experience again during these last weeks in dealing with another aspect of his work. From one point of view I have occasion to be grateful to Dr. Coulton for he has enabled me to reaffirm with renewed conviction that such attempts as I have made to follow up Dr. Lea's trail "have always ended in a most deeply rooted mistrust of every statement made by him."[11]

APPENDIX III
EMMANUEL LE ROY LADURIE

In marked contrast to the vacuous academic credentials of Lea, Professor Emmanuel Le Roy Ladurie writes with all the accouterments of the halls of academe in productive possession of a professorial chair in a prestigious university. Author of *Les paysans de Languedoc* Ladurie is a leading exponent of the *Annales* school of social history. When he wrote *Montaillou, village occitan de 1294 à 1324* in 1975 it was widely heralded as a masterpiece. In 1978 an English version of *Montaillou* was published in the United States to become a best-seller.

The response of the academic community was euphoric. Professor Colin Morris of the University of Southhampton announced: "It is at once an important illustration of a historical methodology and a vivid recreation of a society which has long ceased to exist."[1] Henry Kamen dubbed it an "outstanding anatomy of a medieval village."[2] The littérateur, V. S. Pritchett, penned a lengthy, glowing account of it in *The New Yorker* magazine.[3] Professor John H. Mundy of Columbia University recorded his sentiments: "To applaud a book sold in supermarkets that one wishes one had written oneself goes against the grain, but I wish to praise Le Roy Ladurie's *Montaillou.*"[4] Professor P. S. Lewis of All Soul's College, Oxford, somewhat more balanced in his review, terms it a remarkable book that some will call a masterpiece and some almost a great one.[5] Professor Jeffrey B. Russell of the University of California at Santa Barbara writing in the *Catholic Historical Review* is more forthright. "A careful reading of *Montaillou* will convince the reader that he or she is indeed in the presence of an outstanding example of the historian's art. Ladurie, author of *Les paysans de Languedoc,* and a scholar in the *Annales* tradition, has here produced one of the triumphs of that tradition, a book that can be compared with the work of Braudel and with the celebrated social studies of dissent by Carlo Ginzburg in Italy and Boyer and Nissenbaum in America. *Montaillou* is a superb work of social history . . . ."[6] And the list could continue.

On the strength of such universal acclaim *Montaillou* would seem to be required reading for the scholar and the public alike. "Careful reading" of Ladurie could very well lead to quite an opposite opinion in an objective reader. Professor Lewis notes "Ladurie's eschewing, for instance, of 'scholarly' apparatus in a number of his references (there is even an endearing seventeenth-century air about them), in some of those (is it 'Harvard-system'?) references not appearing in his finding-list, in the lack of index, and, perhaps, above all, in a kind of genuflection to a selection of gurus, Marx included."[7]

A scholarly critique of such a book as Ladurie's requires the perusal of the original Latin edition of Jean Duvernoy's *Le Registre de l'Inquisition de Jacques Fournier, évêque de Pamiers (1318–1325),* (1965), 3 vols., and the French edition (1978), 3 vols., and, since there are some reservations about the accuracy of these editions, the original manuscript itself must be examined, i.e., cod Vat lat. 4030. Of course the English translation of *Montaillou: Cathars and Catholics in a French Village 1294–1324* (1978), along with the original French version *Montaillou, village occitan, de 1294 à 1324* (1975) must also be at hand. In addition the critic must possess a scholar's competence and familiarity with the Medieval Inquisition and contemporary history. Moreover the time and energy thus expended hardly redounds to the productivity of a busy academic who faces the additional problem of finding a learned journal which will publish his critique—conventional wisdom, or as the British have it 'the authorized version' is not readily challenged in editorial rooms.

Leonard E. Boyle, O.P., D.Phil., Oxford; Professor of Paleography and Diplomatics, Pontifical Institute of Medieval Studies, Toronto, Canada, and currently Prefect of the Vatican Library undertook this burdensome and unrewarding task. Admirably qualified for this undertaking Professor Boyle experienced all of the difficulties suggested above.[8] Some measure of his success may be garnered from Professor Eleanor Searle's review of his article in *Speculum:*[9]

> It is not to belittle Mundy's fascinating study of the Toulouse region to end this review by saying that Boyle's paper "vaut le voyage," as Michelin has it. For it is a study of Le Roy Ladurie's *Montaillou,* and it amounts to a devastating picture

of "*mentalité*" scholarship when done without the fastidious care that it in particular requires. The ten "lessons" Boyle draws from his study of *Montaillou* and the documents that are its basis should be taken to heart by all medievalists. But his best summary of Le Roy Ladurie as historian of this village society is, to this reviewer, the most damning thing that can be said of a scholar and the past: ". . . an adroit and gripping storyteller, but there is little or no sense of responsibility in his pages to the people who created his stories" (p. 127). This is very serious, and Boyle's paper should be read seriously and critically. He has convinced this reviewer, but this is a matter upon which scholars must soberly decide.

Professor Boyle reviews the methodology which Professor Ladurie utilizes in ferreting out the data from his source, *Le Registre de l'Inquisition de Jacques Fournier, évêque de Pamiers (1318–1325),* ed. Jean Duvernoy, 3 vols. (Toulouse: Edouard Privat, 1965). Then he examines how Ladurie fashions this information into a narrative whole.

Five points emerge from his examination of Ladurie's methodology in searching for pertinent data from the inquisitorial register:

1. *Respect your sources.* Is this document the whole record, or only part of it? (It is only part of the register). Is the edition well done? (It is faulty and the original manuscript cod Vat lat. 4030 must be consulted). Is the complete testimony of the witness considered? (Retractions by the same witness in the same document are not mentioned).
2. *Index carefully.* Do the pre-designed categories of investigation accurately reflect what the document actually says? (Examples demonstrate that at times they do not).
3. *Do some homework.* Are unfamiliar or unusual texts, phrases or references thoroughly investigated? (A number of instances of faulty references are recorded).
4. *Bear the cast in mind.* Is a full, rounded view of each person in the source given in order to determine the *mentalité* of

the age? ("... there is little or no responsibility in his pages to the people who created his stories." They are treated "as puppets who are jerked about to document a gamut of preconceived headings from body language, childhood, ecology and fate, to libido, morality, magic and religion, to mention only a few.")

5. *Select wisely.* Should all the thousands of index cards be used, or should one be selective? (Overwriting and striving for effect is often at the expense of sober fact, while reducing the French version of 625 pages to 356 pages in the English edition resulted in numerous blunders).

Professor Ladurie wields the data thus derived from the inquisitorial Register into a narrative as a whole and Professor Boyle reviews the main characteristics of this process in action:

1. *Set the scene.* What is said of the main characters, the men and women of Montaillou, who make the depositions? (Nothing). What were the conditions in the prison where the deponents were held? (Says nothing).
2. *Play fair.* Are the beliefs of the Cathar and the deponents described objectively? (Accounts of the Cathars are moving, detailed and friendly, while that of Catholics is harsh and less easily ascertained).
3. *Be circumspect.* What was the reputation and competence of the rural clergy? (Confidence is shaken, e.g., when Ladurie ascribes a deficiency in a priest, who, it turns out, was not a priest at all).
4. *Hold tightly.* In discussing the same event on different occasions is the author consistent? (Confusion is apparent in a number of instances).
5. *Keep your feet on the ground.* Is the evidence used correctly? (In a number of instances the author takes "off into the blue from a speck.")

In his critical analysis of Professor Ladurie's methodology and narration, Professor Boyle details a number of examples under each heading. His critical analysis should be read in its entirety. "Montaillou Revisited: *Mentalité* and Methodology," *Pathways to Medieval Peasants,* ed. J. A. Raftis, Papers in Medieval Studies, 2 (Toronto: Pontifical Institute of Medieval Studies, 1981) 119–140.

NOTES FOR THE FOREWORD

1. Sidney Painter, *A History of the Middle Ages, 284–1500* (New York: Alfred A. Knopf, Inc., 1953), 311.

2. C.N.L. Brooke, "Heresy and Religious Sentiment: 1100-1250," *London University Institute of Historical Research Bulletin* 41 (1968), 122.

3. John H. Mundy, *Europe in the High Middle Ages, 1150-1305* (London: Longman, 1973), 524.

4. Adhémar Esmein, *A History of Continental Criminal Procedure,* trans. by John Simpson (Rothman Reprints, Inc., 1968) Vol. 5. 93-94: "Elsewhere, from the 1300s onward, the Holy Inquisition has a local history of its own within each of the important European nations. In France it soon lost its importance; at the end of the 1500s it is in rapid decline and on the way to ultimate total desuetude. The pursuit of heresy became a *royal and privileged cause,* the cognizance of which belonged to the royal jurisdiction, except when the king pleased to confer it upon the ecclesiastical authority, which sometimes happened in the course of the complex and changing legislation of the 1500s against the Protestants."

   Henry Kamen, *The Spanish Inquisition,* (Meridian, 1975) 140: "From its inception the Inquisition was meant by Ferdinand and Isabella to be under their control and not under that of the pope as had been the case with the medieval tribunal." (141). "The Inquisition as it existed in 1483 and thereafter, was in every way an instrument of royal policy and remained politically subject to the crown." (144): "All members of the *Suprema* (their number was not fixed) were appointed by the king alone. . . ."

   Malcom Barber, *The Trial of the Templars,* (Cambridge University Press, 1978) 44: "At the same time, the means to accomplish a spoliation of the Temple were at hand in the form of the Inquisition, developed by the papacy, but in France controlled by the monarchy."

   Bernard Hamilton, *The Medieval Inquisition,* (New York: Holmes & Meier Publishers, Inc., 1981) 85: "Philip IV had shown that the Inquisition in France had become a tool of the Capetian government, and its place in the kingdom was henceforth assured."

5. Cicero, *De Oratore,* II, 15 (62).

6. G. K. Chesterton, *The Flying Inn,* 127.

NOTES FOR THE INTRODUCTION

1. Yves Dossat, *Hérésis* Revue d'hérésiologie médiévale. Edition de textes - Recherche Centre National d'études Cathares. (June, 1984) No. 2 70–71.

   Grace K. Coughlin, *Western New York Catholic* (June, 1984). Buffalo, New York.

   Lothar Kolmer, *Historische Zeitschrift* B. 239, 673–675. (1984).

Jacques Paul, *Revue d'histoire de l'Eglise de France* (Juillet-Décembre, 1985). T. LXXI, 354–355.

H. Platelle, *Revue d'histoire ecclésiastique* (Avril-Juin, 1985) LXXX, No. 2. 587–588.

Henry Peel, O.P., *Doctrine and Life* Dublin (April, 1986) Vol. 36, 220–221.

A. H., *Nouvelle revue théologique* T. 108, No. 1 (Janvier-Fevrier, 1986) 145.

J. W., *Bulletin de théologie ancienne et médiévale* (Janvier-Décembre, 1986) 118.

Alexander Murray, *History* Vol. 70 (June, 1985) 278–279.

F. Casado, *Estudio Agustiniano* Vol. XX (Septiembre-Diciembre, 1985), Fasc. 3. 583–584. Valladolid.

Thomas Deutscher, *Canadian Catholic Historical Review* (October, 1985) 32/352.

Bernard Schnapper, *Revue historique de droit français et étranger* No. 4 (Oct.-Déc., 1985) 583-584.

Msgr. James P. Connelly, for *The Catholic Standard and Times* Philadelphia.

Gerard G. Steckler, S.J., *Homiletic & Pastoral Review* (October, 1984) 70–71.

Yves Dossat, *Catholic Historical Review* Washington, D.C.: Vol. LXXI, No. 4 (October, 1985) 632–633.

Bernard Hamilton, *Heythrop Journal* Vol. XXVII, No. 1 (January, 1986) 91–92.

Tolle Lege Villanova, 1984.

John Hine Mundy, *Speculum* Vol. 60, No. 2 (April, 1985) 490.

Yves Dossat, *Cahiers de civilisations médiévale X^e-XIIe siècles* XXVIII anné, No. 2-3 (Avril-Septembre, 1985) 297–298. Université de Poitiers, Centre d'études superieures de civilisation médiévale.

Carl A. Volz, *Church History* (June, 1987), p. 271.

2. Walter Ullmann, "Medieval Principles of Evidence," *Law Quarterly Review*. Vol. 62 (1946) 77.

3. Walter Ullmann, "Some Medieval Principles of Criminal Procedure," *Juridical Review*. Vol. 59 (1947) 1-2.

4. Henri Maisonneuve's review of *Historiographie du catherisme* (Cahiers de Fanjeaux, XIV). (Toulouse: Privat, 1979). *Revue d'histoire ecclésiastique*. Vol. LXXVI, No. 2 (April-June, 1981) 386–391. Translated and republished with the kind permission of *Revue d'histoire ecclésiastique*.

NOTES FOR CHAPTER I

1. *The Book of the Two Principles*. English translation in *Heresies of the High Middle Ages*, ed. and trans. by Walter L. Wakefield and Austin P. Evans (New York: Columbia University Press, 1969) 511–591 with notes 790–808.

2. Cf. Bernard Hamilton, "IX. The Cathar Council of Saint-Felix Reconsidered," *Monastic Reform, Catharism and the Crusades (900–1300)*, (London: Variorum Reprints, 1979). 23–53.

3. Deposition of Sybille Sabarethès in *Les Cathares,* ed. R. Nelli, F. Niel, J. Duvernoy, D. Roché (Paris: Editions de Delphes, 1964) 108.
4. *Summa* of Rainerius Sacconi, trans. in Wakefield and Evans, *op. cit.* 330.
5. Ibid., 490–491.
6. Deposition of Sybille Peyre in J. Duvernoy, *Le Registre de l'Inquisition de Jacques Fournier, évêque de Pamiers (1318–1325)* (Paris: Mouton, 1978) II, 582; also II, 408; Vernet in *Dictionnaire de théologie catholique,* I, 679; Wakefield and Evans, *op. cit.,* 743 n. 15.
7. The biblical proofs for the Cathar teachings are taken from *The Summa contra Haereticos, Ascribed to Praepositinus of Cremona,* ed. by Joseph N. Garvin, C.S.C. and James A. Corbett (University of Notre Dame Press, 1958).
8. Marie-Humbert Vicaire, "Les Cathares Albigeois vus par les polémistes," *Cahiers de Fanjeaux* (Toulouse: Privat, 1968), III, 125.
9. Chronicle of Laon, and Walter Map's account in Wakefield and Evans, *op. cit.,* 203.
10. Jean Rousset de Pina in *Histoire de l'Eglise,* ed. A. Fliche and V. Martin, IX, vol. 2, 169.
11. Profession of Faith at Lyons 1180-81 by Valdès in Wakefield and Evans, *op. cit.,* 206ff.
12. J. Gonnet and A. Molnar, *Les Vaudois au moyen âge* (Turin: Claudiana, 1974) 102–103.
13. Rev. H. J. Schroeder, O.P., *Disciplinary Decrees of the General Councils* (St. Louis: B. Herder Book Co., 1937) 237ff.
14. *Contra epistolam Manichaei quam vocant Fundamenti* (V. 6). Eugene Portalié, *A Guide to the Thought of Saint Augustine,* trans. by Ralph J. Bastian, S.J. (Chicago: Henry Regnery Co., 1960) 120.

NOTES FOR CHAPTER II

1. H.-I. Marrou, "L'Héritage de la chrétienté," in *Hérésies dans l'Europe pré-industrielle 11e-18e siècles,* ed. by Jacques Le Goff (Paris: Mouton, 1968) 51ff.
2. John H. Mundy, *Liberty and Political Power in Toulouse 1050–1230* (New York: Columbia University Press, 1954), p. 81f. Also in his *Europe in the High Middle Ages 1150–1309* (New York: Basic Books, 1973), p. 536.
3. Henri Platelle, "Piété et mentalités populaires au XIe siècle," in *L'Eurasie XIe-XIIIe siècles.* vol. VI, 97–135; Canon 3 of Third Lateran Council (1179) and Canon 13 of Second Council of Lyons (1274); Yves Dossat, "Le clergé méridional à la veille de la Croisade Albigeoise," *Revue historique et littéraire du Langue-doc,* 263–278; Leonard E. Boyle, O.P., *Pastoral Care, Clerical Education and Canon*

Law, 1200–1400, (London: Variorum Reprints, 1981), and his "The Constitution "Cum ex eo" of Boniface VIII" in *Medieval Studies,* XXIV (1962) 263–302; Pierre Mandonnet, O.P., *St. Dominic and his Work,* trans. by Mary Larkin, chapters II, XVI, XVII. (St. Louis: Herder, 1944).

4. Letter 221 of St. Bernard in *Les Cathares: documents et articles,* eds. by R. Nelli, F. Niel, D. Roché, and J. Duvernoy (Paris: Delphes, 1964) 11; Innocent III's *Register* Book III in Migne PL vol. 214, col. 904f. and Potthast *Regesta pontificum Romanorum,* II, 1177.

5. Elie Griffe, "Un pays livré aux routiers et aux hérétiques," *Les Débuts de l'aventure Cathare en Languedoc (1140–1190),* (Paris: Letouzey & Ané, 1969) 137ff.; Marie-Humbert Vicaire, " 'L'affaire de paix et de foi' du Midi de la France," *Cahiers de Fanjeaux,* (Toulouse: Privat, 1969), vol. 4, 106ff.

6. Canon 27 of Third Lateran Council in *Disciplinary Decrees of the General Councils,* trans. by H. J. Schroeder (St. Louis: Herder, 1937) 234.

7. Letter of Raymond V, Count of Toulouse in *Les Cathares,* eds. R. Nelli et al. 13; Henri Maisonneuve, *Études sur les origines de l'inquisition,* (Paris, 1960) 130.

8. Canon 4 of the Council of Tours, in J. Mansi, *Sacrorum conciliorum nova et amplissima collectio,* (Florence, 1759–1798), XXI, cc. 1177–78.

9. H. J. Schroeder, *op. cit.* 234.

10. *Corpus juris canonici,* ed. E. Friedberg, (Leipzig, 1879), c. 9, X, V, 7. Vol. II, 780–781. Cf. Maisonneuve, *op. cit.* 155ff.

11. Maisonneuve, *op. cit.* 155ff.; Walter Ullmann, "The significance of Innocent III's decretal *'Vergentis'* in *Études d'histoire du droit canonique dédiées à Gabriel Le Bras* (Paris: Sirey, 1965), Vol. I 729–741, and 81 in his *Principles of Government and Politics in the Middle Ages.*

12. J. P. Migne, *Patrologiae latinae cursus completus,* (Paris: 1844–1855), Vol. II, cc. 903–906.

13. Walter Ullmann, *Principles of Government,* 225f. "That is to say, the approval he (Innocent III) gave to Dominic to do as the heretics did, to provoke in public the population to discussion and to argument as the heretics did, to behave in the same way as the heretics behaved, to roam about in tattered clothing so as to be indistinguishable from genuine heretics - these instructions would show that Innocent was forced to reckon with the multitudes, but, in order to cope with them he turned the movement upside down by leading the multitude instead of permitting it to lead itself."

14. P.L., vol. 214, cols. 172–174; Maisonneuve, *op. cit.* 186ff.; W. Wakefield, *op. cit.* 66; Shannon, *op. cit.,* 17, 33; Mandonnet, *op. cit.* 127.

15. Schroeder, *op. cit.* 236; *Register* Lib. XVI, ch. XXX, cols. 823–826.

16. Schroeder, *op. cit.* 242ff.

17. The best short accounts of the Albigensian Crusade in English are Austin P. Evans, "The Albigensian Crusade," *A History of the Crusades,* eds. R. L. Wolff & H. W. Hazard (Philadelphia: U. of Pennsylvania Press, 1962), Vol. II, ch. 8, and Robert

J. Kovarik, "The Albigensian Crusade: A New View," *Studies in Medieval Culture,* III. ed. by John R. Sommerfield (1970) 81–91. A longer work in French: Pierre Belperron, *La Croisade contre les Albigeois et l'union du Languedoc à la France, 1209–1249,* (Paris: Plon), 2nd ed., 1948. The two best contemporary chroniclers were Peter of Vaux de Cernay, *Historia Albigensis,* new translation by Pascal Guébin and Henri Maisonneuve (Paris: Vrin, 1951), and William Tudela, *La Chanson de la croisade Albigeois,* trans. by Eugene Martin-Chabot (Paris: 1931) *Les Classiques de l'histoire de France au moyen âge,* vol. 13. Cf. Hefele-Leclercq, *Histoire des conciles,* V. 3 1492–1495; Bernard Hamilton, VIII. "The Albigensian Crusade," *Monastic Reform, Catharism and the Crusades (900–1300),* (London: Variorum Reprints, 1979). 1-40; Henri Platelle, "La Croisade des Albigeois," *L'Eurasie XIe-XIIIe siècles.* Vol. VI. 319-323.

18. William of Tudela, *op. cit.* 86–89.
19. Cf. Christine Thouzellier in Fliche et Martin, *op. cit.* vol. X 303; Shannon, *op. cit.* 110-111.

NOTES FOR CHAPTER III

1. Lucien Auvray, *Les Registres de Gregoire IX.* No. 539. (Bibliothèque des Écoles Françaises d'Athènes et de Rome). 3 vols. Paris, 1896–1910.
2. Ibid. no. 540.
3. *Monumenta Germaniae Historica,* Leges, sect. 4, vol. II, 196.
4. *Cupientes,* in J. Mansi, *Sacrorum conciliorum nova et amplissima collectio,* vol. XXIII, cc. 185–186. 31 Vols. Florence, 1759–1798.
5. Thomas Ripoll, *Bullarium ordinis fratrum praedicatorum.* vol. I, p. 47, nos. 71 & 72. 8 vols. Rome, 1779–1790.
6. Bernard Gui, *Practica inquisitionis hereticae pravitatis,* edited by Célestine Douais, 232–233. Paris, 1886.
7. Theodore de Cauzons, *Histoire de l'inquisition.* Vol. II, p. 86. 2 vols. Paris, 1909, 1912.
8. Elphège Vacandard, *The Inquisition,* trans. by Bertrand L. Conway, C.S.P., 87. (New York, 1949); Henri Maisonneuve, *op. cit.* 261; A. Potthast, *Regesta pontificum Romanorum, inde ab anno post Christum natum 1198 ad annum 1304,* vol. I, no. 9041. 2 vols. Berlin, 1874, 1875.
9. Discussed in Chapter Four.
10. Ibidem.
11. Ibidem.
12. Ibidem.

13. Adhémar Esmein, *A History of Continental Criminal Procedure,* trans. by John Simpson (South Hackensack, New Jersey: Rothman Reprints, 1968), vol. V, 79.

14. Questions and answers from cod Vat lat. 4030, courtesy of the Vatican Library and the Pius XII Memorial Library, Saint Louis University. This manuscript has been edited by Jean Duvernoy, *Le Registre de l'inquisition de Jacques Fournier, évêque de Pamiers (1318–1325),* (Toulouse: Privat, 1965). 3 vols., and translated into French and annotated by the same author (New York: Mouton, 1978), 3 vols. The Bishop of Pamiers acted as his own Inquisitor. In 1314 he became Pope Benedict XII.

15. Peter Maury was a shepherd of Montaillou in the diocese of Pamiers and came from a household of Cathar heretics.

16. Cf. Chapter One, 10. Also Jean Duvernoy, *op. cit.* III, 348, 349, 460, 461, 471, 527, 530, 532, 535, 537, 561, 574, 575, 584, 881, 882, 939, 975, 990, 1019, 1125, 1126, 1139, 1140, 1142.

17. *The Chronicle of William of Pelhisson,* translated by Walter L. Wakefield, *Heresy, Crusade and Inquisition in Southern France, 1100–1250* (Berkeley: University of California Press, 1974) 211–212.

18. Sentencing posthumously is a phenomenon not confined to the Middle Ages. According to the N.Y.TIMES, December 26, 1984, A 21, date line Los Angeles, Dec. 25 "A state judge has scheduled a hearing for next month to decide whether a man who died after he was convicted of murdering his wife and son should be given a life sentence so that his heirs from a previous marriage will not inherit nearly $1 million in insurance money."

19. A good example of these manuals for inquisitors is that of the Inquisitors Bernard of Caux and John of St. Pierre prepared in 1248/9 at the request of Innocent IV and the Archbishop of Narbonne, and translated by Walter Wakefield, *op. cit.* 250–258.

20. Élie Griffe, *Le Languedoc Cathare et l'Inquisition (1229–1329),* (Paris: Letouzey & Ané, 1980) 115ff; Yves Dossat, *Les Crises de l'inquisition toulousaine au XIIe (1233–1273),* Bordeaux: Bière, 1959) 172, 324, 336; A. Molinier, *L'Inquisition dans le midi de la France: Étude sur les sources de son histoire,* (Paris, 1890) 18 note 3.

21. The citation C. 17, *de haereticis,* V, 2, in VI° is an abbreviation for Chapter 17 of the decretals of Pope Boniface VIII concerning heretics Book 5, title 2.

22. C. 20 *de haereticis,* V, 2, in VI°.

NOTES FOR CHAPTER IV

1. Maurice Bévenot, S.J., "The Inquisition and its Antecedents," *The Heythrop Journal,* 7 (1966) 386–7.

   H.-I. Marrou, "L'Héritage de la chrétienté," *Hérésies et Sociétés dans l'Europe pré-industrielle 11e-18e siècles,* 51–57.

Walter Ullmann, *Law and Politics in the Middle Ages,* 146–7:

"The consideration of canon law as a source of governmental ideas necessitates some remarks on a feature with which the modern world is not unfamiliar. The elimination of activities held to be subversive of the existing social order is a governmental activity in a number of modern societies. In the Middle Ages the extermination of heretics was of profoundest concern to virtually all Western governments, precisely because in the overwhelming majority they were built on theocratic foundations. Hence attacks on these bases by unorthodox views publicly expressed affected the very core of Rulership. The sources relating to the public prosecution of heretics are of a varied nature, but most are easily accessible in governmental decrees by emperors, popes and kings. These legislative measures might be termed applied governmental jurisprudence. Leaving aside Justinian's example of burning books by decree, there were the legislation of the Lateran Councils, the joint imperial-papal decree of Frederick Barbarossa and Lucius III in October 1184, the legislative measures taken by Innocent III, and the edicts issued by Frederick II in November 1220. The important substantive point was the juristic conception of heresy as high treason. The procedural measure — the Inquisition — was partly the extension of the ancient episcopal visitation, partly the adaptation of late Roman procedural principles, and partly rested upon the conception of heresy as a public crime. What needs stressing in this context is that these sources reveal the character of society and its government far better than any learned tract could have done: they show that the custody of the ideologically cementing bond of society lay in ecclesiastical hands which only goes to show the ecclesiological substance of society."

Ullmann, *The Individual and Society in the Middle Ages,* 36. With the permission of the Johns Hopkins University Press.

"Here some specific observations are called for regarding the medieval thesis of the corporational structure of society, rooted as this was in Roman conceptions. Students of medieval history are familiar with the trite postulate *Utilitas publica prefertur utilitati privatae.* In drawing attention to this medieval maxim, I am well aware of the resuscitation of this very same maxim in more recent days, but we should not forget that a considerable span of time has intervened between the medieval application of the principle and its modern revival. The significance of this principle in the medieval period is that what mattered was the public weal, the public welfare, the public well-being, in brief, the good of society itself, even at the expense of the individual well-being if necessary. If we were to try to pursue the matter a little further, we would understand on the one hand why the law played so crucial a role in the Middle Ages, for law, in order to be law, is at all times addressed to the generality, and on the other hand the very real concern of medieval governments for safeguarding the interests of society, that is, the public good, which was considered to be the *supremum bonum.* From this consideration arose the demand for suppressing publicly all individual opinion contrary to the assumptions upon which society allegedly was built."

2. Cf. Chapter One.

3. Cf. Henri Maisonneuve, "Le droit romain et la doctrine inquisitoriale," *Études d'histoire du canonique dédiées Gabriel Le Bras,* t. II, 931–942.

4. Walter Ullmann, "Medieval Principles of Criminal Procedure," *Juridical Review,* Vol. 59 (1947) 4–5:

   "In medieval times two methods were employed to bring a criminal to justice, and both methods were ultimately derived from Roman Law. The one was the ancient accusatorial principle, directly borrowed from Roman Law, and the other was the inquisitorial principle, adapted to the needs of the time by way of contemporary interpretation of relevant Roman passages. The principle that was recognized throughout the medieval period as the only ordinary method of bringing a criminal to justice was accusatorial: it was, as every teacher stressed, the *"remedium ordinarium."* The inquisitorial method, to be sure, was never heartily embraced by the civilians, and it was always recognized as the *"remedium extraordinarium."*

   This accusatorial principle consisted in the right of every citizen to accuse another citizen before the ordinary, competent judge. But this right to prosecute entailed the duty of the State to protect the citizen against calumnious accusations; this care for the individual found expression in the Roman regulation that the accuser must "subscribe" to the punishment which he had proposed for the accused — that is to say, the accuser, in the so-called "subscriptio," (D.48.2.3. and 7.1; D.48.10.28; C.IX.45.3.) undertook to suffer the very same punishment for the very same crime with which he charged the accused, in the event of a failure to furnish complete proof of the guilt of the defendant. The writ, or the "libellus," to be a valid and formal accusation, had therefore to contain the "subscriptio in crimen."

   "Moreover, if the accused was taken into custody, the accuser too had to share in the deprivation of liberty." (5).

   "For what accuser was reasonably certain that he would be successful with his accusation? And what accuser could be expected to have that amount of public spiritedness and idealism not only to risk heavy penalties, but also to undergo imprisonment before the trial? That this requirement of a "subscriptio" in the "libellus" acted as a brake and a deterrent to otherwise justifiable prosecutions is self-evident: the ordinary citizen became discouraged from filing accusations. The inevitable result was that crimes were left unpunished and the security of the public was gravely imperilled." (10–11).

5. John C. Glynn, *The Promoter of Justice,* (Catholic University Press, 1936) 5: "The Romans with their hereditary attachment to formalism never conceived of a public personality who might prosecute in the name of society but adhered to the ancient system of popular accusation to the end." Cf. A. Esmein, *op. cit.* 80. Cf. Walter Ullmann, "Medieval Principles of Criminal Procedure," *Juridical Review.* Vol. 59 (1947) 24 note 1. Baldus, *loc. cit.,* no. 2: "Fama habetur pro persona accusatoris." Nearly all jurists employed this phrase.

6. Walter Ullmann, *Principles of Government and Politics in the Middle Ages.* 200:

   "We have seen how in the pursuit of the theocratic theme Louis IX introduced the inquisition under the cover of public necessity and maintenance of peace and order. The introduction of the Romano-canonical inquisitorial procedure, too, was only an off-shoot of the maxim that truth must be investigated *ex officio.*"

7. James A. Hughes, *Witnesses in Criminal Trials of Clerics* (Washington, D.C.: Catholic University Press, 1937) 29.

8. "Not only the testimony of the witnesses but also their names must be made known to him, that he may be aware who testified against him and what was their testimony; and finally, legitimate exceptions and replications must be admitted, lest by the suppression of names and by the exclusion of exceptions the boldness of the defamer and the false witness be encouraged." Canon Eight of the Fourth Lateran Council, trans. by H. J. Schroeder, O.P., *Disciplinary Decrees of the General Councils* (St. Louis: B. Herder Book Co., 1937) 249.

9. Theodore de Cauzons, *Histoire de l'inquisition en France* (Paris, 1912), II, 193–194.

10. A. Esmein, *op. cit.*, 90, 92, 129; R. Van Caenegem, "The Public Prosecution of Crime in Twelfth-Century England," *Church and Government in the Middle Ages*, eds. C. N. L. Brooke, D. E. Luscombe, (Cambridge University Press, 1976) 70.

11. A. C. Shannon, *The Popes and Heresy in the Thirteenth Century* (Villanova, Penna.: Augustinian Press, 1949) 77–78; also "The Secrecy of Witnesses in inquisitorial tribunals and in contemporary secular criminal trials," *Essays in Medieval Life and Thought* (New York: Columbia University Press, 1955) 66. "It is pertinent to recall, in this connection, that even in enlightened England it is only since 1836 that persons accused of felony have been able to avail themselves of the assistance of Counsel, or see copies of the depositions made against them," Cecil Roth, *The Spanish Inquisition* (1937) reprinted by W. W. Norton, 1964, 89.

12. Canon three of the Fourth Lateran Council, 1215.

13. James A. Hughes, *op. cit.* 29. Cf. King Louis IX's instructions to his *Enquêteurs* in 1247:

   ". . . . insuper ad audiendum et scribendum et ad inquirendum *simpliciter et de plano* de injuriis et exactionibus, serviciis indebite receptis ceterisque gravaminibus, si qua facta sunt aliquibus sive allata per baillivos nostros, praepositos, forestarios, servientes vel familias eorumdem, tempore regni nostri, et ad injungendum praedictis vel eorum heredibus ut ipsi restituant ea ad quorum restitutionem per ipsorum confessiones vel per probaciones viderint predicti Fratres ipsos secundum Deum teneri." *Recueil des Historiens des Gaules et de la France* (Paris, 1898ss. Vol. XXIV, 4, preface) as quoted by Alexander Wyse, O.F.M., "The *Enquêteurs* of Louis IX," *Franciscan Studies*, vol. 25 (March, 1944) No. 1, 56. Cf. Walter Ullmann, *Principles of Government and Politics in the Middle Ages*, 196, note 1: "By the late thirteenth century they had changed their names from *enquêteurs* to that of *réformateurs.*"

14. Nicholas Eymeric, *Directorium inquisitorum*, ed. F. Pegna (Venice, 1607), Tertia pars Directori, 317 D, 446:

   "De defensionibus reorum . . . Et sic concedentur sibi advocatus, probus tamen, & de legalibus non suspectus, vir utriusque juris peritus, & fidei zelator: & procurator pariforma, ac processus totius copia, suppressis tamen testium, & deponentium, ac accusantium nominibus, ubi Inquisitor in conscientia sua videat eisdem grave periculum imminere, si ipsorum nomina proderentur propter potentiam delatorum. Ubi autem non videatur tale periculum imminere, si ipsorum nomina proderentur propter potentiam delatorum, sunt hujusmodi nomina delato in praedicta copia exprimenda, juxta c. Statuta de haeret. lib. 6." Cf. Douais, *op. cit.*, 184; Shannon, *op. cit.*, 78–79; Walter Ullmann, "The Defence of the Accused in the Medieval Inquisition," *The Irish Ecclesiastical Record*, vol. 73 (1950) 481–2:

"The summary character of the inquisition ordered by Pope Boniface VIII left all possibilities of legal aid untouched. Canonistic scholarship was unanimous in its demand that the accused must not be deprived of legal aid. For the canonists recognized that inquisitorial proceedings, deciding as they did life and death and possibly the salvation of the accused, should be conducted in such a manner that all possible legal objections, remedies and defences might be employed to save an individual from the not infrequently harsh sanctions of the law. But what defendant charged with the crime of heresy was conversant with the legal subtleties and niceties that might prevent him from being delivered to the executioners? The rule was that, if after careful admonition the defendant had pleaded guilty, he was considered to have forfeited his right to legal help: but if he denied committing any heretical action, which was, of course, the normal reply to the charge, the inquisitor was bound to grant him legal aid in the person of a qualified advocate, even if there were no explicit petition for his help: *Si autem post tres monitiones reus negat se umquam haereticum fuisse, tunc advocatus ei dandus est, etiam not petenti.* The defence was looked upon as an integral part of the proceedings: *Judices providere debent, ut advocatus adsit, ne reus defensionis careat.* For the inquisitors ought not only to be judges in the strict meaning of the term, but also the *patres reorum.*"

15. Raoul C. Van Caenegem, "Public Prosecution of Crime in the Twelfth Century England," *Church and Government in the Middle Ages* (London: Cambridge University Press, 1976) 41–42.

16. 'Ordeal' derives from the Anglo-Saxon *ordal* meaning judgment. In the Middle Ages it was synonymous with *jugements de Dieu, judicium Dei* from the prevailing belief that God intervened in these trials, and this belief was common to all countries.

17. There seems to be somewhat of a difference of opinion in this matter, for some writers claim as above, that the innocent sank, e.g., Eugene Moriarty, *Oaths in Ecclesiastical Courts* (Washington, D.C.: Catholic University Press, 1937) 15, whereas Timothy J. McNicholas, *The Septimae Witness* (Washington, D.C.: Catholic University Press, 1949) 8 asserts just the opposite, namely that the innocent floated! The matter is academic today, but could have caused some confusion at the time!

18. Cf. John W. Baldwin, "The Intellectual Preparation for the Canon of 1215 against Ordeals," *Speculum* (October, 1961), vol. XXXVI, no. 4, 613–636.

19. Eugene Moriarty, *op. cit.*, ix.

20. John H. Langbein, *Torture and the Law of Proof* (Chicago: University of Chicago Press, 1977) 7 © 1976, 1977 by the University of Chicago.

21. *Ibid.*, 12ff. Professor Langbein examines the safeguards minutely.

22 *Bullarium diplomatum et privilegiorum sanctorum Romanorum pontificum,* ed. by A. Tomasetti (Turin, 1857, 1874), III, 556.

23. Walter L. Wakefield, *op. cit.*, 179:

"How were the confessions obtained? The use of torture in the inquisitorial process had not yet appeared. The scrutiny of the very few references to it in Languedoc before 1250 and, indeed, until nearly the end of the century, reveals that torture was the action only of secular officials who were dealing with heretics without reference to the Inquisition."

Jean Français et Michel Massie, "Une grande famille au temps de la crise Cathare: Les Morlanne béarnais et les Morlane carcassonnais," *Bulletin de littérature ecclesiastique,* Janvier-Mars, 1984, 20:

"Quant à torture, elle ne laisse point de trace dans les registres de l'Inquisition, de 1250 à 1258, au temps de l'épiscopat de Guillaume Arnaud."

Yves Dossat, *op. cit.,* 215:

"Une fait demeure sûr: rien, jusqu'aux environs de 1260, ne permet d'affirmer que la torture ait été employée par les inquisiteurs méridionaux."

Élie Griffe, *Le Languedoc Cathare et l'Inquisition (1229–1329),* 26:

"Dans la riche documentation que nous possédons pour toute la seconde partie du XIIIe siècle, il est difficile de relever, au course de l'instruction des procèces, des cas torture imputables aux juges d'Église."

P. 271 in regard to Jacques Fournier, Bishop and Inquisitor at Pamiers, whose inquisitorial Registers are used in Chapters One and Three above:

"Ce n'est pas lui qui aurait usé de la torture, même à l'égard des plus obstinés. Tout au plus se servait-il de la prison préventive pour arriver à les faire parler."

Célestin Douais, *Documents pour servir à l'histoire de l'inquisition dans le Languedoc* (Paris: 1900) ccxxxviii:

"La *Practica* de Bernard Gui est muette au sujet de la torture."

P. ccxl: "Pour le Languedoc, cette affirmation est certainement outrée. La prison, telle était la voie de contrainte ordinairement employé. C'est le seul moyen d'obtenir l'aveu qui apparaisse soit dans le registre du greffier de l'Inquisition de Carcassonne, soit dans les *Sentences* de Bernard Gui; c'est le seul moyen d'aveu que Bernard Gui énonce dans la *Practica.* Et par là les inquisiteurs du Languedoc donnaient la main aux inquisiteurs d'outre-Rhin."

Georgene W. Davis, *The Inquisition at Albi, 1299–1300* (New York: Columbia University Press, 1948) 34 says that the sentence of Guillelmus Cavalerii contradicts Douais' above assertion. Since Douais himself edited Bernard Gui's *Practica* it is incredible that he was not aware that Gui mentioned torture. Guiraud noted that Gui speaks so briefly of torture that it may rightly be concluded that he did not make much use of it. In this regard Lea asserts that torture was freely and ruthlessly applied. In trying to substantiate such pronouncements Georgene Davis claims that she is sure of one instance of torture, i.e., the above mentioned Cavalerii. On the other hand, J.-L. Biget, "Un procès d'inquisition à Albi en 1300," *Le Credo, la morale et l'inquisition,* Vol. 6 of *Cahiers de Fanjeaux,* 291 states that "Trois au moins des prévenus d'Albi ont donc été soumis à la question."! It is interesting to note that Bernard Gui's *Practica* was a compilation of formularies in use for the various actions of the tribunal: Letters of Commission, Methods of Citation, Method of Abjuration, Form of Oath, Formula of Interrogation, Form of the Sentence for those released to the Secular Arm, etc., since these must be pronounced in a definite legal form. Thus the formula was presented as a model with a space left open for inserting the name of the person involved. Arguing from the amount of time elapsing between their first appearance before the tribunal and the second or third Davis reasons "If this change of heart was the result of pressure as charged, the shorter interval undoubtedly looks like application of the question: the longer, however, suggests imprisonment." (p. 36). Biget, on the other hand, calculates that if the confession comes in the shorter period, it implies a voluntary confession, whereas the elapsing of a longer period suggests the use of torture (290–291)!

24. John H. Langbein, *op. cit.*, 138. Torture in Renaissance England.
25. Adhémar Esmein, *op. cit.*, vol. 5, 630.
26. Tarde, *Penal Philosophy,* as quoted by Esmein, *op. cit.*, V, 629.
27. Herbert Radtke, "Torture as an Illegal Means of Control," *The Death Penalty and Torture,* ed. by Franz Bockle and Jacques Polier (New York: The Seabury Press, 1979) 4. Cf. also "Annual Report 1976–77" *Amnesty International;*

    The London Sunday Times, June 19, 1977.

    William Borders of the New York Times reported that a judicial commission that investigated Northern Ireland's prisoners concluded today that there were indications that an unspecified number of suspected terrorists there had been tortured during police questioning. The panel, headed by former Crown Court Judge Harry Bennett, and including a former police official and a doctor, recounted indications of "bruising, contusions, hyperextension and hyper-flexion of joints, hair-pulling, jabbing, rupture of the ear drums and increased mental agitation." (New York Times, Saturday, March 17, 1979. sec. III, 4).

NOTES FOR CHAPTER V

1. Walter L. Wakefield, *op. cit.* 179; Yves Dossat, *op. cit.* 249, 261, 263.
2. Jean Guiraud, *Histoire de l'inquisition au moyen âge,* (Picard, 1935), II, 146.
3. Cf. Henri Platelle, "La purification: Le Pèlerinage," *L'Eurasie XIe-XIIIe siècles,* 115–119.
4. Today bulldozing houses of Arabs is a common practice of the Israeli, e.g., September 11, 1982, *New York Times*; October 5, 1983 *Washington Post,* A1 and A28; November 12, 1984, "Israelis Destroy Houses of 28 West Bank Arabs", *New York Times:* "Jerusalem, Nov. 11 — Twenty-eight crude houses belonging to Palestinian farmers in the West Bank were demolished by Israeli authorities today as 'illegal structures.' "

    "The action brought to nearly 80 the number of such houses destroyed in the last 10 days, according to Elice Shazar, spokesman for the Civil Administration, the Israeli authority that governs the occupied territories."; March 20, 1985, *Washington Post,* A1 and A16: "When they were unable to find Shehadi, the Israelis got a bulldozer and destroyed the home of his father. Later, Israeli Army officials said the house that was destroyed contained weapons. Observers from the U.N. Interim Force in Lebanon, who were in the village throughout the search, said, however, that no weapons were found in the house," etc., etc.
5. Yves Dossat, *op. cit.*, 267, 318.
6. Frederick W. Maitland and Frederick Pollock, *The History of English Law,* (Cambridge, 1898), II, 452.

7. Jean Duvernoy, *op. cit.*

8. Maitland, *op. cit.*, II, 453.

9. Annik Porteau-Bitker, "L'Emprisonnement dans le droit laïque au moyen âge," *Revue historique de droit français et étranger,* vol. 46 (1968) 390–428; "la prison pour crime n'est établie que pour la garde des criminels pendant l'instruction de leur procès et non pour les punir . . . suivant cette maxime: Nam hujusmodi poenae interdictae sunt carcer enim ad continendos homines, non ad puniendos haberi debet . . ." (390); "En droit canonique l'emprisonnement est donc une peine temporelle, la seule peine afflictive à la disposition des officialités et même la plus grave quand elle est perpétuelle. S'opposant aux peines vindicatives, l'emprisonnement est considéré comme une peine médicinale, un remède largement utilisé dans le seul but de racheter, d'amender les délinquants; il vise donc à corriger autant qu'à punir les coupables." (391).

   Walter Ullmann, "The Defence of the Accused in the Medieval Inquisition," *The Irish Ecclesiastical Record,* vol. 73 (1950) 486–7: "Imprisonment can have two functions: either the prevention of flight of the defendant before the trial, or punishment after the sentence had been passed. Whilst the civil laws permitted imprisonment only as a means of custody, the canon law also allowed it as a form of punishment." "The most frequent form of imprisonment was a kind of 'house arrest,' that is to say, the accused was confined to his dwellingplace or to the locality within which he lived, or to the whole district." (488).

10. Yves Dossat, *op. cit.*, 273.

11. Louis Halphen, *L'Essor de l'Europe (XI-XIIe siècle),* (Paris: Presse Universitaire, 1948) 328.

12. L. Tanon, *Histoire des tribunaux de l'inquisition en France,* (Paris: 1893) 482-483.

13. Yves Dossat, *op. cit.*, 247–268. Many of the relevant documents are contained in Célestin Douais' *Documents pour servir à l'histoire de l'inquisition dans le Languedoc,* (Paris, 1900), 2 vols.

14. Yves Dossat, *op. cit.*, 261, 263; also his article "Une figure d'inquisiteur: Bernard de Caux," *Cahiers de Fanjeaux,* VI, 261ff.

15. Yves Dossat, *op. cit.*, 267, 268; Walter L. Wakefield, *op. cit.*, 193.

16. *Times Literary Supplement,* Thursday, June 9, 1966, in review of *Le Registre de l'inquisition de Jacques Fournier.*

17. Adhémar Esmein, *op. cit.*, vol. 5, 10.

18. Albert C. Shannon, *The Popes and Heresy in the Thirteenth Century* (Villanova, Penns.: The Augustinian Press, 1949) 122ff.

19. Cf. Chapter Three, 93ff.

20. John Henry Wigmore, *A Panorama of the World's Legal Systems* (Washington, D.C.: Washington Law Book Co., 1928, 1936) 955–956.

21. Walter Ullmann, "Medieval Principles of Evidence," *Law Quarterly Review,* vol. 62 (1946) 77: "Furthermore, by the time of the classical period of the medieval jurists, that is in the fourteenth century, new ideas had been brought to bear upon the practice

in the Courts, through the recognition of canon law as a source which, at least theoretically, had equal authority with that of the *Corpus Juris Civilis*. And, lastly, the practice of the ecclesiastical Courts evolved principles which were bound to react upon secular Courts, just as canonistic theory reacted upon the doctrines of the civilians. This theoretical and practical interplay resulted, then, in the establishment of certain fundamental principles which influenced Western legal thought to a very marked degree."

NOTES FOR APPENDIX II

1. *Henry Charles Lea* A Biography by Edward Sculley Bradley (Philadelphia: The University of Pennsylvania Press, 1931) 40.
2. Ibid., 42, with the permission of the University of Pennsylvania Press.
3. *Father Thurston* A Memoire with a bibliography of his writings. By Joseph Crehan, S.J. (Sheed and Ward, 1952)—some 760 items, and 180 articles in *The Catholic Encyclopedia* and several books.
4. *Father Thurston* by Joseph Crehan, 121. The reference to Lord Acton is in regard to Acton's requesting Lea to write the Chapter on "The Eve of the Reformation" for the *Cambridge Modern History*. The "Dr." with which Thurston prefaces Lea's name refers to the Honorary Doctorates conferred on Lea by a number of universities late in his life; he possessed no earned degrees.
5. *The American Catholic Quarterly Review* Vol. XXVIII July, 1903 No. 111, 417–434.
6. Coulton's letter to Thurston of November 2, 1936. *Month,* p. 52 January, 1937, vol. 169.
7. *Ibid.,* 53. E.g., "By way of specimen, the concluding words of Dr. Coulton's letter of November 14th may suffice. He writes: 'It is idle for you to plead that the slander is now thirty-three years old. If it was true then, it is equally true now, if (as I confidently assert) it is now grossly false, then you have been thirty-three years before the world with this falsehood upon your conscience.' "
8. Crehan, *op. cit.* 155.
9. "I have a little shilling booklet of mine: 'Some inexactitudes of Mr. G. G. Coulton,' (Sheed & Ward, 1927). See especially p. 41 of the booklet in question." *Month,* 53.
10. "Dr. Coulton and Dr. H. C. Lea. A Challenge and Its Sequel." Herbert Thurston in the *Month* January, 1937. 53–54.
11. Ibid., 128. In this regard it might be pertinent to cite Walter Ullmann, holder of the Chair of Medieval History at Cambridge University: "It is, indeed, remarkable that some of our modern historians, notably Lea, and, largely following him, the late Dr. G. G. Coulton, hardly ever refer to the canon law, and if they do, the relevant Bull or decree of a pope or of a council is quoted in a manner which is apt

to convey a totally misleading impression." ("The Defence of the Accused in the Medieval Inquisition," *The Irish Ecclesiastical Record* June, 1950. Vol. 73, No. 8, 481). Similarly, Thurston makes the comment: "Dr. Lea understands as little of Canon Law in general and the workings of the Penitentiary in particular as the average Frenchman does of the procedure of the English House of Commons; but his critics unfortunately know less than himself, and when he dogmatises they accept him at his own valuation." ("Dr. H. C. Lea on the causes of the Reformation," *The American Catholic Quarterly Review* Vol. XXVIII. July, 1903. No. 111, p. 421 n. 5.) The other article which Father Thurston criticized and also offered to expose ten palpable blunders — and which Coulton chose to ignore — remained in the *Cambridge Modern History* for over a half a century.

NOTES FOR APPENDIX III

1. *History* (February, 1979) 85–86.
2. *The London Tablet* (April, 1979) 377–378.
3. *The New Yorker* (February, 1982) 128–130.
4. "Village, Town, and City in the Region of Toulouse," *Pathways to Medieval Peasants,* ed. J. A. Raftis, 141.
5. *The English Historical Review* (1977) 371–373.
6. *Catholic Historical Review* (1980) 678–680.
7. *English Historical Review* (April, 1977) 372.
8. Leonard E. Boyle, O.P., "MONTAILLOU REVISITED: *Mentalité* and METHODOLOGY," *Pathways to Medieval Peasants,* ed. J. A. Raftis, *Papers in Medieval Studies* 2 (Toronto: Pontifical Institute of Mediaeval Studies, 1981), 119–140.
9. *Speculum* (January, 1984) 199.

SELECTED READINGS

Manuscript: cod Vat lat. 4030.

Amnesty International. "Annual Report 1976–77." *Torture in the Eighties.* Amnesty International, 1984.

Auvray, Lucien, *Les Registres de Gregoire IX,* 3 vols. (Paris, 1896–1910).

Baldwin, John W., "The Intellectual Preparation for the Canon of 1215 Against Ordeals," *Speculum* (October, 1961), vol. XXXVI, No. 4, 613–636.

Berkhout, Carol T., and Jeffrey B. Russell, *Medieval Heresies: A Bibliography 1960–1979.* (Toronto, 1981).

Bévenot, Maurice, S.J., "The Inquisition and its Antecedents," *The Heythrop Journal,* 7 (1966).

The Book of the Two Principles. Translated in *Heresies of the High Middle Ages,* by Walter L. Wakefield and Austin P. Evans. (New York, 1969).

Borst, Arno, *Die Katharer* (Stuttgart, 1953). French translation by Charles Roy (Paris, 1978).

Boyle, Leonard E., O.P., "Montaillou Revisited: *Mentalité* and Methodology," *Pathways to Medieval Peasants.* Ed. J. A. Raftis (Toronto, 1981).

_________, "Innocent III and Vernacular Versions of Scripture," *Bible in the Medieval World.* Studies in Church History. Subsidia 4.

_________, "Popular Piety in the Middle Ages: What is popular?," *Florilegium.* Vol. 4 (1982) 184–193.

Brooke, C. N. L., "Heresy and Religious Sentiment: 1100–1250," *London University Institute of Historical Research Bulletin* 41 (1968).

Bullarium ordinis fratrum praedicatorum, ed. Thomas Ripoll, 8 vols. (Rome, 1779–1790).

Bullarium diplomatum et privilegiorum sanctorum Romanorum pontificum. Ed. A. Tomasetti (Turin, 1857, 1874).

Cahiers de Fanjeaux

vol. 2 *Vaudois languedociens et Pauvre Catholiques.*

vol. 3 *Cathares en Languedoc.*

vol. 4 *Paix de Dieu et guerre sainte en Languedoc.*

vol. 6 *Le Credo, la Morale et l'Inquisition.*

vol. 11 *Le religion populaire en Languedoc du XIIIe siècle à la moitié du XIVe siècle.*

vol. 14 *Historiographie du Catharisme.*

vol. 15 *Le pèlerinage.*

vol. 20 *Effacement du Catharisme? (XIIIe-XIVe siècle).*

Les Cathares, ed. R. Nelli, F. Niel, J. Duvernoy, D. Roché (Paris, 1964).

The Chronicle of William of Pelhisson. Trans. by Walter L. Wakefield, *Heresy, Crusade and Inquisition in Southern France, 1100–1230.* (Berkeley, 1974).

Corpus juris canonici, ed. E. Friedberg (Leipzig, 1879).

Davis, Georgene W., *The Inquisition at Albi 1299–1300.* (Columbia University Press, 1948).

De Cauzons, Theodore, *Histoire de l'inquisition,* 2 vols. (Paris, 1909, 1912).

Dondaine, Antoine, O.P., "Le registre de l'Inquisition de Jacques Fournier. A propos d'une édition récente," *Revue de l'histoire des religions.* Vol. 178 (1970) 49–56.

Dossat, Yves, *Les Crises de l'inquisition toulousaine au XIIIe siècle (1233–1273),* (Bordeaux, 1959).

__________, *Eglise et hérésie en France au XIIIe siècle.* (London: Variorum Reprints, 1982).

Douais, Célestin, *Documents pour servir à l'histoire de l'inquisition dans le Languedoc,* (Paris, 1900).

Duvernoy, Jean, (ed.) *Le Registre de l'inquisition de Jacques Fournier, évêque de Pamiers 1318–1325,* (Toulouse: Privat, 1965), 3 vols. Translation into French (Paris: Mouton, 1978).

Emery, Richard W., *Heresy and the Inquisition in Narbonne.* (Columbia University Press, 1941).

L'Eurasie XIe-XIIIe— siècles. Vol. VI *Peuples et Civilisations,* eds. Georges Duby et Robert Mantran (Presses Universitaires de France, 1982).

Esmein, Adhémar, *A History of Continental Criminal Procedure.* Translated from the French by John Simpson (South Hackensack, N.J., 1968).

Études d'histoire du droit canonique dédiées Gabriel le Bras. (Paris: Sirey, 1965). 2 vols.

Evans, Austin P., "The Albigensian Crusade," *A History of the Crusades.* Eds. R. L. Wolff & H. W. Hazard. (Philadelphia, 1962). Vol. II, Ch. 8.

Glynn, John C., *The Promoter of Justice* (Washington, D.C., 1936).

Gonnet, J. and A. Molinar, *Les Vaudois au moyen âge.* (Turin, 1974).

Griffe, Élie, *Les Débuts de l'aventure cathare en Languedoc (1140–1190).* (Paris, 1969).

_________, *Le Languedoc cathare de 1190 à 1210.* (Paris, 1971).

_________, *Le Languedoc cathare au temps de la Croisade (1209–1229).* (Paris, 1973).

_________, *Le Languedoc cathare et l'inquisition (1229–1329).* (Paris, 1980).

Grundmann, Herbert, *Bibliographie zur Ketzergeschichte des Mittelalters (1900–1966).* (Rome, 1967).

Guiraud, Jean, *Histoire de l'inquisition au moyen âge.* (Paris, 1935).

Gui, Bernard, *Practica inquisitionis hereticae pravitatis.* Ed. Célestine Douais. (Paris, 1886).

Halphen, Louis, *L'Essor de l'Europe (XIe-XIIIe siècle).* (Paris, 1948).

Hamilton, Bernard, *The Medieval Inquisition.* (New York, 1981).

Histoire de l'Église. Eds. A. Fliche and V. Martin. 26 vols.

A History of the Crusades. Eds. R. L. Wolff and H. W. Hazard. (Philadelphia, 1962).

Hérésies et sociétées dans l'Europe pré-industrielle 11e-18e siècles. Ed. Jacques Le Goff. (Paris, 1968).

Hughes, James A., *Witnesses in Criminal Trials of Clerics.* (Washington, D.C., 1937).

Kovarik, Robert J., "The Albigensian Crusade: A New View," *Studies in Medieval Culture.* Ed. John R. Sommerfeldt. III. 81-91. (1970).

Lambert, Malcolm, *Medieval Heresy, Popular Movements from Bogomil to Hus.* (New York, 1977).

Langbein, John H., *Torture and the Law of Proof.* (Chicago, 1977).

Maisonneuve, Henri, *Études sur les origines de l'inquisition.* (Paris, 1960).

__________, "Le droit romain et la doctrine inquisitoriale," *Études d'histoire du droit canonique, dédiées à Gabriel Le Bras.* (Paris, 1965). II, 931-942.

Maitland, Frederick W. and Frederick Pollock, *The History of English Law.* (Cambridge, 1898).

Mandonnet, Pierre, *St. Dominic and His Work.* Trans. by Mary B. Larkin. (St. Louis, 1944).

Mansi, J., *Sacrorum conciliorum nova et amplissima collectio.* 31 vols. (Florence, 1759–1798).

Migne, J. P., *Patrologiae latinae cursus completus.* 221 vols. (Paris, 1844–1855).

Molinier, A., *L'Inquisition dans le midi de la France: Étude sur les sources de son histoire.* (Paris, 1890).

Monumenta Germaniae Historica. Leges, sect. 4. vol. II.

McNicholas, Timothy J., *The Septimae Witness.* (Washington, 1949).

Moriarty, Eugene, *Oaths in Ecclesiastical Courts.* (Washington, 1937).

Mundy, John H., *Liberty and Political Power in Toulouse 1050–1230.* (New York, 1954).

__________, *Europe in the High Middle Ages 1150–1309.* (New York, 1973).

Painter, Sidney, *A History of the Middle Ages.* (New York, 1953).

Peter of Vaux de Cernay, *Historia Albigensis.* Eds. and trans. Pascal Guébin and Henri Maisonneuve. (Paris, 1951).

Peters, Edward, *Heresy and authority in medieval Europe: documents in translation.* (University of Pennsylvania Press, 1980).

Porteau-Bitker, Annik, "L'Emprisonnement dans le droit laïque au moyen âge," *Revue historique de droit français et étranger,* vol. 46 (1968).

Potthast, A., *Regesta pontificum Romanorum, inde ab anno post Christum natum 1198 ad annum 1384.* 2 vols., (Berlin, 1874, 1875).

Radtke, Herbert, "Torture as an Illegal Means of Control," *The Death Penalty and Torture.* Eds. Franz Bockle & Jacques Polier. (New York, 1979).

Shannon, Albert C., *The Popes and Heresy in the Thirteenth Century.* (Villanova, 1949).

_________, "The Secrecy of Witnesses in inquisitorial tribunals and in contemporary secular criminal trials," *Essays in Medieval Life and Thought.* Presented in honor of Austin Patterson Evans. (Columbia University Press, 1955).

The Summa Contra Haereticos Ascribed to Praepositinus of Cremona. Eds. Joseph N. Garvin and James A. Corbett. (Notre Dame, 1958).

Schroeder, H. J., O.P., *Disciplinary Decrees of the General Councils.* (St. Louis, 1937).

Tanon, L., *Histoire des tribunaux de l'inquisition en France.* (Paris, 1893).

Tarde, "Penal Philosophy," as quoted by A. Esmein, *A. History of Continental Criminal Procedure.* Vol. 5, 629.

Ullmann, Walter, "The Defence of the Accused in the Medieval Inquisition," *Irish Ecclesiastical Record.* 73 (1950) 481–489.

_________, "Some Medieval Principles of Criminal Procedure," *Juridical Review.* Vol. 59 (1947), 1-28.

_________, "Medieval Principles of Evidence," *Law Quarterly Review.* Vol. 62 (1946), 77–87.

_________, "Reflections on Medieval Torture," *Juridical Review.* Vol. 56 (1944), 123–137.

Vacandard, Elphège, *The Inquisition.* Trans. Bertrand L. Conway. (New York, 1949).

Van Caenegem, Raoul C., *Methods of Proof in Western Medieval Law.* AWL[S]K Academiae Analecta. (Brussel, 1983).

———, "The Public Prosecution of Crime in Twelfth-Century England," *Church and Government in the Middle Ages.* (London: Cambridge University Press, 1976).

———, "The Law of Evidence in the Twelfth Century," European Perspective and Intellectual Background. *Proceedings of the Second International Congress of Medieval Canon Law,* ed. Stephen Kuttner and J. Ryan (Vatican, 1965).

Van der Vekené, Emil, *Bibliographie der Inquisition. Ein Versuch.* (Hildesheim, 1963).

Vernet, F., "Albigeois," *Dictionnaire de théologie catholique.* I, c. 679.

Wakefield, Walter L., and Austin P. Evans, *Heresies of the High Middle Ages.* (Columbia University Press, 1969).

Wakefield, Walter L., *Heresy, Crusade and Inquisition in southern France, 1100–1250.* (University of California Press, 1974).

Walther, Daniel, "A Survey of Recent Research on the Albigensian Cathari," *Church History.* 34 (1965), 146–177.

Wigmore, John Henry, *A Panorama of the World's Legal Systems.* (Washington, D.C., 1928, 1936).

William of Tudela. *La Chanson de la croisade albigeoise.* Ed. & trans. by Eugene Martin-Chabot. (Paris, 1931). *Les Classiques de l'histoire de France au moyen âge.* Vol. 13.